Ignite Your Light
&
Awaken Your Soul

This book is designed to clarify and provide helpful reference information for those who have an interest in psychic studies. The information contained within this book it not intended to be used for any form of alternative or complimentary therapy or for any medical diagnosis.

Ignite Your Light
&
Awaken Your Soul

Elly Charles

Published in 2021 by Welford Publishing

ISBN: Paperback 978-1-9162671-6-9

Front cover design © Fuzzy Flamingo
Editor: Christine McPherson
Front cover and author photograph © Natasha Holland

A catalogue for this book is available from the
British Library.

I am dedicating this book to my beautiful Grandma, Meryl Auwdsley Watson, who forever remains my biggest champion. Thank you for the guidance, the messages and the continued connection from the afterlife that you bring to me to help me to stay ever spiritually connected.

Grandma thank you for guiding me to pick up the pen to write. I know you are proud of what I have written.

I am also dedicating this book to my mother Jennifer Diane Charles who has always been such a huge supporter of everything I do. Mum thank you for always having faith in me and for teaching me all the wisdom and spiritual knowledge that I now carry forward in my life.

I am dedicating this book to all of our family's ancestors for they are who encouraged me and inspired me to write it, forever your energy lives on in our family name and our energy line. We continue forward with your energy for eternity even after each physical form has passed through to the afterlife, the positive powerful energy of you remains.

Contents

Introduction

Hello and welcome! You might be wondering what led you to pick up this book? Or what exactly you want to achieve by reading it. Perhaps you find yourself feeling lost in a cloud of confusion, trying to search into the depth of your soul about why you are here on this earth, and this might just be the book to help you.

Perhaps you have found yourself hearing or feeling strange things, or even seeing things that do not feel of this world. Perhaps you have always questioned what type of spiritual being you are. Maybe you have always had a keen interest in spiritual aspects, yet you didn't know where to go or even how to start learning more. Did you ever find yourself predicting the future? Maybe you were full of questions that were never being answered.

Perhaps you're worried that you were a bit crazy, so you kept it to yourself because you worried that others would think you were strange. Maybe you were brought up to believe that when people die, they are gone and that is it. Then what next? NOTHING? Yet the thought that there is nothing after death just doesn't sit right with you. Perhaps you have always believed in the afterlife and have wanted to explore it more, but thought only special people have that gift. Maybe you have lost someone really special to you and have always longed to believe that they are there. Or have you thought you have felt or seen them since their passing, but then shrugged it off because you didn't have physical proof?

Maybe you have felt blocked by the things that have gone on within your life. Do you feel like your past holds you back? Maybe you're someone who suffers with depression, or who has been stuck in a dark hole for a while, losing hope. Or perhaps you are someone who has managed to get out of the hard times that held you back, and now you are on a new track looking for an amazing spiritual upgrade.

Wouldn't it feel amazing to understand your psychic senses? Wouldn't it feel truly freeing to be in control of your life in a whole new way? Exploring your enlightenment rather than being afraid of it. Having that clear knowing that you are now on the right path and that these strange sensations are ACTUALLY not strange at all. Knowing why these psychic things are really happening, and learning how to use your senses in the correct way. Wouldn't it be amazing to use your senses to help others?

I completely understand that all these feelings, thoughts, and questions, can all feel a bit overwhelming at times.

Let me take you back...

I found my deeper understanding of spirituality through the sheer hunger to understand exactly why certain things were happening to me and around me.

How did I know such random things? How did I see spirit and hear them? How did I become strong within my truth as a spiritual being??

Questions, questions, questions! I asked constant questions to my guides within meditation, and I let it all unfold like a shining light in front of me, highlighting the way.

You see, I was once lost and alone within my mind, not knowing why I was really here. I used to feel like a waste of space, yet now I feel like I *own* my space, and I fill it up with pure light and love. How do you feel so good within yourself, you might ask. How do I now know my true calling in life? And how can you get to that feeling yourself? Well, my friend, keep reading and you will find out.

Along my journey I have seen, heard, and felt some seriously amazing, crazy, scary, and unbelievable things. I have spoken to thousands of souls who have passed over. I have even helped souls to pass over properly, or to pass on their messages to their loved ones still here. This is my most favourite thing to do. My heart fills with so much love when I connect to these lovely souls and listen to their story. Yet it wasn't always so easy for me; at times, it was scary and very draining. Like you, I had so many questions and never seemed to get the answers. Whenever I would ask people, they would look at me like I was crazy. Luckily, I was from a spiritual family, so I did have support. However, none of us knew just how psychic I would really become.

I am so passionate about sharing my knowledge with you because I have experienced first-hand and listened intently to the guidance from my ancestors of what, how, when, and why certain things happen in our lives. And it's actually in our darkness that we grow stronger; through our pain we become positive power. It's through transition and our lost days that we find ourselves along a path that ignites into an awakening, and we finally understand and see the way.

You see, I was so hungry to understand why and how my senses worked, and why they are in my life, that I began to create my own techniques within psychism and mediumship and used them within my own hobbies. When I eventually turned this into a business, I found that my techniques began to strengthen. This brought me more and more clarity, as well as a growing reputation in bringing significance and accuracy to my spiritual readings. When I connected to people's loved ones, the messages I was receiving were so in-depth that they resonated with every single person I read for. I found that even when people were more interested in having psychic guidance about their futures, months down the line they would be coming back to tell me that everything I had told them had come true. I watched my five-star positive recommendations come in by the day, along with more and more bookings, and I knew for certain that this was truly my calling.

You might be thinking, 'Oh well, it's ok for you.' But believe me, it has not been an easy journey. I will be sharing some of my real-life experience throughout the book, but just so you know that we are on the same page – literally – I feel guided to share this with you.

Oh, my fucking life, I cannot do this. I'm going to die… are the thoughts running through my mind as I stand at the edge of a plane, 15,000 feet in the air, strapped to a man who has done this hundreds of times before and has no fear; it's just simple to him!

As I find myself being shuffled closer and closer to the edge of this open door, all I can see are the clouds down below, but there is no time to change my mind. For fuck's sake, Elly, why are you doing this in the first place? Just get a grip.

Then suddenly I'm free-falling at the speed of 160 miles per hour. Falling through the sky, I realise why people do this. In that 60 seconds of free-falling, all those fears leave me, and I realise that I'm ok. In fact, I'm better then ok. I'm ALIVE, fully and truly alive – and everything is fucking fantastic!

That moment I was fearing so much was the moment I took the next step to conquering a huge fear of mine. Of course, heights are something many people struggle with, but it wasn't really the fear of heights that was holding me back. It was the fear in my mind that I couldn't do it.

Yes, how many of us have had this fear of 'I cannot do it'? Isn't it crazy that such thoughts can hold us back?

So, those 60 seconds of free-falling proved to be the ultimate moment for me to realise exactly what I have truly achieved in the last three years, and particularly in the last nine months.

You see, over these last few years I have achieved so much in my spiritual journey, which led me to create a wonderful business that I love so much, called Light After Life. Better yet, my transformation has now led me to achieving physical things that I use to find limiting – like jumping out of a plane.

Six months ago, I climbed a temple in the middle of a Mexican jungle, and yet again extreme anxiety was holding me back. Halfway through the climb, I looked down and realised I was above the jungle trees and this old temple was just getting higher and higher. I somehow managed to get up to the top, and they were right. It was worth it. Yes, because it was so beautiful and peaceful, but more so because I had actually achieved it. I HAD DONE IT.

So, how did I get from having a drug addiction, absolutely no money, and suffering with severe depression, to now flying freely through the sky, achieving and experiencing amazing activities and places, and helping hundreds of people all over the world.

Let's go back to when I was 26, had just moved home, and was in the process of getting clean from my cocaine addiction. Living in this tiny little flat in a town I didn't know, I had shut myself off from all the people I knew, and in a way shut myself away from my own life. I was left to pick up the pieces of the destruction I had caused for so long. No-one was interested in helping me any more, because I had burnt my bridges with everyone. My photography business had failed, and I had no money. In fact, I owed lots of money to so many people.

The deep, heavy feelings so rooted inside of me pulled me back, yet I knew I had to trust in something. That something was the light. This light my mum had always told me about, the light from my angels, the light that sang to my soul. And I just had to believe that something was going to change.

As I locked myself away, realising I had nothing, I began to focus on this pure white light which grew stronger and stronger. I'd always had strong spiritual senses, so I knew what was happening. Little did I know, however, that this light would be what changed my life forever and was the beginning of a massive transformation that has brought me to this new and wonderful life that now flows so freely.

When I was in my cloud of depression, I would cut myself in-between my thighs just so I could get this pain out. I would look in the mirror and be disgusted with myself at the way I had intoxicated and abused my body so badly over the years.

I now know that everything which held me back in life was simply pain I felt from my upbringing, and mainly from sexual abuse as a child. This had created a huge stench bomb of self-destruction that later caused me to have serious blocks in all areas of my life, including my career.

If I'm honest, I never felt like I fitted in. No matter what job I had, it just didn't feel right. I always felt unfulfilled, and often felt sick at the thought of even going into work. When I became fed-up with working in dead-end jobs, I tried to set up a photography business and it did go well at times. However, because of my party life and drug-taking, it never worked out. I was always more interested in getting fucked. WHY? To take the pain of my past away. But of course, I didn't realise that back then.

Eventually, my photography business became non-existent. Don't get me wrong, I was still a brilliant photographer, but it just didn't feel right. It didn't excite me. I began to meditate more and more in my little flat, on my own, and over the months I found that instead of wanting to cut myself and tell myself horrid things, I began to tell myself that I loved myself. I was focusing on that light I saw and trusted. I started to become aware of loved ones that had passed over, sitting with me and showing themselves to me. They looked so beautiful and glowing. I could hear them, and they brought me comfort. When they started to show me little snippets of my future, I would ask them to guide me, and I gave thanks to them for healing me.

Little by little, I began to venture out of my flat, feeling stronger and stronger. Slowly but surely, things started to change, but it took three years from deciding to get clean to realising that I felt like a new woman. Our pain goes deep, and we have to peel the layers back, but I found that so many layers were being healed at different stages. It was difficult to confront, but this light was keeping me going.

Now I understand why I had to go through so much hard work and pain. I am a light worker and I needed to have these lessons in life to be able to clear this out and understand what it's like to truly heal myself, so that I can help to heal and guide others.

Fast forward three years from that little flat. I was now 29 years old, living in a new home with my almost two-year-old daughter. A single mum, I was heartbroken over the split with my daughter's father and feeling very lost. I had two choices: go back to intoxicating myself and going downhill, which at that time was very tempting – when you have had an addiction, there is always a part of it that remains with you; or actually listen to this pull to the spiritual realm, which I felt so strongly.

Thankfully, I was strong and listened to that pull. I was already in spiritual development circles and decided to start offering readings for people, in return for a small donation. I would spend three hours in the evening, when my daughter was in bed, focusing on practising reading people's energy and connecting to spirit linked to them. Very soon, people that I was practising on began to tell their friends about me, and I had people I didn't know contacting me for readings.

I decided to start charging a set fee of £15 per person, and once this was going well, I found myself drawn to set up a business page, then to register my business. The name I chose for my business was Light After Life, because it felt right within my heart. Through my mediumship, I realised I had a beautiful connection with souls passed over, and a great deal of respect for spirit. I saw that their light still shone so brightly even though their physical form had gone, and again the light that I trusted in so much felt important to include in my business name.

So when I created the name, I was listening to my soul and respecting spirit, because I am a messenger to help connection through different light beings earth-bound and passed over, to continue forward. I felt I was pumping so much positive energy into my business when I chose the name, and I still do.

Within the first seven months, I had received over one hundred five-star reviews on my business page, but even then, I still didn't realise just what I had achieved. All I knew was that I really enjoyed giving readings for people, and the significance I got from spirit blew me away. I began to realise that I was doing this because I was helping people, but it was helping me and my pain, too.

One year into offering the readings as a spiritual service,

I set up a class. This was something that my grandmother, who is my lovely spirit guide, had been showing me in visions and telling me I needed to sort out. However, it took me about four months to finally listen to her and actually do it. When I did, I thought it would just be a little circle, similar to the ones I had attended myself a few years previously. But I was over the moon to find that seventeen people had booked on the first class, and I was overwhelmed that so many had turned up. That class turned from one class into eight separate classes in different locations, which still run now.

During that next year, I learned how to teach and what to teach, and how to understand people from a teacher/student basis, but this was a HUGE turning point for my career and my interaction with other people. There were times when I felt very energised and excited, but there were also times when I felt stressed and found I was going above and beyond to help people which left me no time to just be with my heart. It proved to be another big part of my lesson, though, to make sure that what I am doing always feels good for me.

One year into teaching and two years into setting up Light After Life, it began to dawn on me that people actually wanted to hear what I have to say. *Fuck! People trust me*, I thought. It might sound silly, but that realisation was so profound because I realised that even though I was doing a good job and felt good about my work, until then I had still been holding onto a belief that I was worthless.

When I realised this, it gave me a great boost, not in an egotistical way but in a really authentic, genuine way. This helped me to transform my business even more and allowed both sides of my business grow. I had started to expand the business online, offering one-to-one sessions for students who did not want to be in a group setting, so I was teaching people all over the world. People were coming from left right and centre to have readings with me or to be taught by me.

Since then, I have created The School Of Spirituality, which focuses on helping members to trust in their intuition and find their true purpose along their spiritual path, as well as focusing on psychism and mediumship. I am very proud of this membership.

You see, what I have realised through meeting and teaching so many amazing people, is that everyone has a story to tell. Some of us might get stuck and be that way for a long time; some of us might never get through it. But some of us find a way to move through it and even forgive the ones that hurt us. The ones who abused us or lied to us.

When you forgive, you set yourself free. And that is what I did. I forgave. I realised that, through my pain, I found my power. Through my readings, I gave people the space to just be. Through my teachings, I helped others to overcome their pain and to realise that they are not crazy.

Understanding why certain things have happened in your life is the biggest lesson of all. Now, through all the feelgood vibes of creating my business, I had raised my vibration to a higher level without realising it. As a result, I was finding more and more positive people coming into my life and more positive opportunities appearing. Doors were opening and I was being recognised for the work I was doing, which was simply just my TRUTH of who I was. I was even nominated in the *Soul & Spirit* magazine awards, and ended up being placed as one of the finalists.

I started to accept that there really is something in this' believe and you shall receive' stuff. I found that financially I was doing a lot better, and I was able to heal the old money patterns I'd had from way back during my drug-taking days. Now, instead of worrying about finances, I believed that my spirit guides would help me get along in life. Money is just a transfer of energy, and I'm not greedy, but I was finally accepting that YES, I DO DESERVE MONEY. The money I received from my work, I put straight back into my business to help it progress even further. And I happily pay out for other services or bills now, because I know money will come back.

Everything is a transfer of energy. Absolutely everything.

In February 2020, another psychic told me that two years ago I would never have imagined achieving all that I have. The comment shook me, because I realised he was absolutely right. I cry with joy at how far I have come and what I have achieved. From that young girl who was so messed up by the mistakes of adults around me, to the drug-intoxicated young woman that was still so fucked-up trying to heal her inner child, I am now a soulful woman loving life. But knowing my roots and where I've come from always helps me to be on top of who I am as a woman.

People have their contracts in life, and it's down to us to accept and acknowledge our contracts. As I said, it's through our pain that we can find positive power, and I saw that in the white light that I decided to trust all those years ago. That light kept me going. It got brighter and brighter, and through the darkness I shone. I decided to RISE. I took on my contract.

I feel so lucky that I was guided to create a business that sings to my soul and lifts so many up in a positive way. It's not a job to me, it's my life; my business is ME.

For anyone out there who feels lost, who feels stuck within the trauma of their past, who questions if they can ever get through this, just know that you have your light, too, and you CAN find it. Your light is waiting to guide you. Switch it on, because this is your truth.

Your light is your soul, and your soul has work to do.

Find your path and do what you are destined to do.

Believe and you shall RECEIVE…

Amidst all of this, I was still just being me – Elly, a fun, glowing person who now trusts in my authenticity to see me through anything in life. My name and my teachings were reaching people all over the world, and I found myself in situations where things just fell into place.

I was invited to be guest speaker at many fabulous events, and doors were opening left, right, and centre, to better my business but also my self. For me, my journey led me to create a spiritual business, but for others it can take you to whatever destiny is waiting for you. Whatever, whoever, and wherever your path takes you, it's still YOUR JOURNEY. The one that is waiting and is absolutely right for you.

Those that have been taught by me know that my true passion is for the spirit world. Passing on the knowledge that I have learnt is a part of my calling, because I am a messenger. I've been given a job and it's to help others find their spiritual path, whatever that may be, then to guide them into strengthening their spiritual skillset. Seeing people have those amazing lightbulb moments and realising that they aren't actually crazy, is just mind-blowing to me. Being with people when they are giving to others, by using the techniques that I have helped them to understand, feels so amazing, and I am just so excited to continue sharing all that I have learnt and all that I have created to anyone who is ready and dedicated to learn. My heart bursts with watching people learn, grow, and heal.

You see, when you listen to your senses and you wake up to who you truly are, everything flows, and you know exactly what you have to do and when to do it. Divine intervention will take place.

So, I ask you: are you ready for your spiritual upgrade? Are you excited to learn and grow? Are you ready to ignite your light?

In this book, I will be sharing with you the special techniques I have created to explore in depth each clairsensory that you have within your energy stream. Through these theories and techniques, you will start to discover what's really going on for you and how it's happening, you will learn how to be fully protected and grounded throughout, so you start to gain more and more control of your spirituality, transforming from a submissive psychic into a mental psychic.

You will gain a clear insight to what your next steps are and who in the spirit world is guiding you. You will know the difference between psychism and mediumship, and be able to use your clairsensory for both, or individually. The abilities are limitless with the knowledge you will learn.

I will also guide you to start using your newfound spirituality in other areas of your life. Once you understand

and make tracks onto your true purpose path, you will see just how amazing you truly are and the type of results you will gain. I guarantee that after reading and practising the techniques, you will look back and understand just why you picked this book up. You will be clear on exactly what your next steps are. You will not feel lost any more.

As with everything I do, this book is written intuitively. If you are wondering why some chapters are longer than others, it's because that's what my guides told me to write!

Are you ready for the next step on your journey?

I understand how you feel. I've been there, and I'm ready to guide you. I'm with you every step of the way and would be honoured to guide you along your spiritual journey. I am so touched that you bought my book, now let's make you LOVE my book and LOVE your journey.

Through the darkness, there is always light. And the light always, always WINS. You will see the way.

This is your journey and I'm so excited for it to unfold.

Here comes your spiritual upgrade. Ready?

Let's ignite your light!

Elly x

P.S. Make sure you get yourself a super special notepad, as I will be asking you to complete some exercises as we go. They will astound you.

P.P.S. Some of the exercises will require you to work with a partner, but don't worry if you're reading this alone. You can save those exercises for another time. It will be the perfect reason to meet up with one of your spiritual friends.

Chapter 1

How I Discovered the Clairs

Where do I begin with all this clairsensory chit-chat? Well, well, well, and my, my, my, comes to mind. I will begin by sharing how I came about understanding the different clairs. If you're anything like me, you will have found yourself feeling very, very confused with what is going on within your mind and body. And if your anything like me, you have even felt pretty scared about what you think feel or see? Maybe you have been left in the dark, not understanding your sensory system that flows within your energy stream.

How do you understand what is going on within your energy?

How can you be prepared for a psychic message or a connection from spirit?

How can you trust that what you're seeing, hearing, feeling, etc, is true? Perhaps you worry that you will look like an absolute nutter if you tell people what you're really feeling.

Yep, I experienced all of that as well, including the bad dreams and the overwhelming feelings of things I just couldn't explain. I used to find myself waking up each day

– or sometimes not sleeping each night – feeling so drained. By that point, I knew that I was psychic and that I could communicate with spirit. I felt so eager, through absolute exhaustion yet sheer determination, to fully understand just exactly HOW and WHY I was able to communicate with spirit and why I knew so many things about people's past and futures. I began to ask so many questions around this.

How do I feel this pain one feels? How do I see spirit? How do I hear spirit? Why do I get such a strong knowing, with no doubt in my mind that it's correct? How? How? How? And why me? Elly Charles, who had been so lost in life before?

That was when I began to explore my senses to find out the connection behind this. Of course, I had learnt a little about the clairs through some of my spiritual trainers and from my family, but it wasn't enough to understand them in depth. What I began to realise, through asking so many questions in my mind and from researching and reading, was that clairvoyance didn't actually mean that I was psychic. The real meaning of clairvoyance is 'clear seeing'. So, I began to explore this further with a host of questions. If it's purely for clear seeing, how come I hear spirit? How can I smell spirit and feel them? How is this working within me?

As I began to learn more and more, I started to put what I was learning into my reading sessions, and practised every single day on my clients and on my family and friends. I began to ask people to send me images of loved ones passed over, and I started to speak to the people in the photos. I would ask the photos what they wanted to tell me, and I would assess exactly how my body was feeling. You see, you have to be extremely aware of your own energy that's true to you. Because if you are not fully aware of your own energy and how it works within your body, you will not always be picking up on spirit around you. Nor the energy around you.

I also began to understand the difference in using clairs for spirit connections and for people who are alive, how the energy came in, and how different clairs triggered for different types of souls and people. I realised that through really assessing exactly what my mind and body was doing, I had a whole lot going on, and it became more and more known to me how each clairsensory was working. I now knew that this psychic energy I was feeling no longer seemed like this big ball of things that I experienced without having a bloody clue why. Instead, it was actually a step-by-step process each time, and that each one was different in the way the connection happened.

I was able to understand so much more because I was now understanding the clairs within me and what each one was providing me. How amazing is it to hold seven clairsenses and be able to access them all? I was so excited by this and would sit at my lovely kitchen table for hours, exploring the things I was seeing, hearing, smelling, tasting, feeling – and I knew something amazing was happening.

I also realised that not only did knowing the clairs help me with understanding messages from spirits connecting, and others who were still alive, but using my clairs for my own life was kicking in. So naturally, as I developed more into understanding the clairs, the messages from my passed-over loved ones became much stronger and clearer, and spirit guides' signatures started to be created with my ancestors that I had never physically met. And it turned out they had a whole lot to say, which was rather fun and enlightening – but also very loving.

My life started to improve so much with regards to my emotions. I had come out of a long clearing healing process that had lasted about three or four years, in which I had carried so much pain from sexual abuse as a child and domestic abuse relationships as a young woman. My previous drug addiction was also part of what I needed to clear and heal during that four-year process.

It was fucking heavy and dark. During that time, I'd had many encounters with spirit, and unfortunately some rather nasty dark ones, too. Of course, intoxicating myself kept me in a lower vibrational frequency, which meant that my energy was not protected and had gaps and holes for spirit to attach and drain me often. I was a shell of a person and didn't know who the fuck I was, or what I wanted in life. In fact, I didn't want to be alive.

So, when I speak of grounding and protection techniques these days, I sure as hell know what I'm doing, because it was having so many draining experiences with spirit that finally led me to really taking this protection and grounding stuff seriously. When I was younger, I used to say to my mum, 'Oh shhhh, I don't need to do that.' But actually, I really DID need to do those things to look after my spiritual wellbeing. Unfortunately, I was rather more interested in partying, and being young I just wanted to try and have fun and cover up the pain from my childhood. However, the drugs eventually stopped being fun, and my life became a big, dark hole of shit where I felt very lost for what seemed like forever.

My clearing/healing process went through stages. It took about a year just to get through the first stage, which was understanding the impact of the destruction I had caused to myself and to others around me. The second year was letting go and healing from the pain and guilt I felt from that destruction, and now really confronting what had gone on in my childhood that had led me to feel so lost. During this time, I was very sad and lonely, and really felt very empty, but I did start to have very strong connections to one of my spirit guides. I didn't realise at the time that she was actually a guide for me, but it felt good to speak to her in my mind and ask her to help me.

Gradually, over the third year of my healing process, I began to come to terms with a lot of my past, and I forgave myself. I also allowed the spiritual connections in more, and that is around the time when the clairs really started to kick in and I felt that hunger to learn about them. This led me into a fourth year of the clearing/healing process, which saw the creation of my spiritual business. For some of that time, I was very confused, because I resisted the spirit realm a lot even though I knew my spiritual senses were so strong. I definitely did not know that I was going to be a medium and a spiritual teacher, and I most certainly did not know that I would be successful with it or even write a book about it.

This all happened when I was around 28-29 years old. I had been a photographer during most of my twenties, and I thought I still wanted to be a photographer and keep my photography business afloat, even though it was really not going well at all. Don't get me wrong. I created amazing images, but I just didn't have the business mind for it, nor even the motivation.

I had experienced so many strange, funny, and even dark spiritual experiences that I was not in any way wanting to be a medium. I had already had many years of psychic experiences. Yet I knew in my heart now that this was part of my path, and no matter how much I tried to ignore it, the calling to listen was too strong and my senses were too intense to ignore, especially when I was getting so much correct and helping people with the messages I received.

So, I started to offer readings more and more to friends of friends, which is what led me to my business, Light After Life. I chose the name because the word LIGHT means everything to me. It's so powerful, and represents our souls, while the rest of the name represents the fact that our souls go on. Just because the physical has passed over, doesn't mean that our spirit body has gone. We are ever more, and our soul moves through each life forever. So, I felt very connected to this name.

As I was giving more readings, I found that more people were contacting me through recommendations, and things just went from zero to 100 in the speed of light. I decided to let go of the photography, and accepted that was not for me any more, as my psychic work was growing into a full-time occupation.

One year into my business, I set up a spiritual development circle which quickly sold out, and this lasted for two years. From that, I went on to run eight physical classes and take on another teacher who could help with running the spiritual classes. I added in one-to-one spiritual development sessions, which I still continue to offer. I found that I was being invited to speak at events and teach large numbers of people, I was offered opportunity after opportunity, and my teachings and readings were being requested from people or professionals in other countries.

I realised that studying the clairs, and how they were helping me to truly assess the messages from my guides or helping me to see my future, was such a beneficial way of really letting myself be guided and seeing how my life unfolded. At times, I had asked my guides, 'But why now? If I'm so psychic and getting such strong significance, then why did I feel so lost? Why did I not see my future?' This intrigued me, but the response I received from my guides was that I had needed to first learn the important lessons of clearing, healing, forgiveness, and trusting in my path. And if they had shown me everything beforehand, I most likely would have not believed it.

I had to truly clear myself out so that I could then become a channel for psychic and mediumistic connections to help others. You see, you can't truly help others if your own shit is in the way. Yes, you can care about people, but you are unable to wholly and truly support them in that moment of need. That's when I realised that I had finally found my purpose – to help others through my spiritual skillset. It felt so good providing people with the comfort, love, clarity, and significance they needed in their life. And it is still the number one thing that keeps me going through my business, knowing that somehow each day I am helping others.

I understand that being looked after by your guides brings rewards like happiness, success, clarity – as well as financially – and I found myself changing into the most beautiful, calm, positive being, allowing myself to flow and be fully guided. Through this, I wanted to really zone in on the clairs, to help my students and clients to really gain a deeper understanding to each clair and how they ignite, and how we can each enhance and strengthen our clairs.

We all have doubts in life, but you must never let the cloudiness of your logic get in the way. You must always trust what is ahead, even if you don't know what it is yet. I didn't know because I was so stuck in a shit, dark hole. My message to you today is that you don't know what is around the corner, but if you're ready to explore it, you will be so amazingly shocked at what you find. Open your mind, open your source, but most of all, open your heart and TRUST it, because your life is about being true to your heart and letting the truth in your heart shine.

Chapter 2

Clairvoyance – Clear Seeing

Clairvoyance (/klɛər'vɔɪəns/; from French clair meaning 'clear' and voyance meaning 'vision') is the ability to gain information about an object, person, location, or physical event, through extrasensory perception.

The most common assumption people make about clairvoyance is that this holds all the psychic senses and values. I used to find myself rather irritated when I would go to see some psychics performing on platforms. Although they were good mediums, I felt they were not in fact demonstrating any clairvoyance at all in the way they were connecting to spirit or the audience's energy.

As I explained earlier, I am a strong believer that knowing the individual clairs inside out has created such a strong foundation for my psychism and mediumship, and the way in which I teach has helped many others create a brilliant foundation for their own spirituality.

Clairvoyance is simply clear seeing – the ability the use sight to connect to spirit. Now, to explore this in more depth, there are two different aspects of Clear Seeing:

1. Internally Seeing

   This includes every type of visual within your mind, and this is the most common form of clairvoyance. Examples of this would be:
   Dreaming
   Out-of-body Experience
   Meditation Visuals
   Visions
   Premonitions & *Déjà vu*
   Memories
   Flashbacks
   Seeing colours, shapes, or symbols within the mind
   Auras within your mind

   This can be used within psychism or mediumship, which I will go into in more detail a little later on. You don't have to be a medium to use clairvoyance.

2. External Seeing

   This includes every type of seeing outside of your physical form. Examples of this would be:
   Seeing auras of people, animals, plants, and objects, with your eyes open
   Seeing energy within the atmosphere
   Seeing spirit within our outside surroundings
   Seeing objects moving around
   Seeing shadows

Seeing flashes of light
Seeing orbs

Again, these external sensations can be used within psychism and mediumship, but you do not have to be a trained medium to externally see.

There is a lot to cover here, so I have broken this down into sharing internal clear seeing in this chapter, and external clear seeing in chapter three.

You do not need to be aware of your psychic senses or mediumship senses at all, but as I mentioned earlier, you may well experience many of these clairvoyance sensations within your body or energy sensory, and it will most definitely benefit you to understand fully just what is happening with your internal and external clear seeing. When you start to understand the difference in each part of clear seeing, you will begin to create the foundations of your spiritual energy, better understand what is going on for you, and KNOW that you are definitely not crazy.

Some of you will be reading this and have found yourself resonating with that list above; perhaps you have already outlined the types of clear seeing you are already aware of. Others may be thinking that you definitely don't get much clear seeing, if any at all. Don't worry. I am sure you will understand your level of clear seeing once I have explained in more depth how each part of it works.

How various parts of clear seeing starts to happen for each individual can vary, depending on the individual's awareness. Our lives and how we have lived can also have an impact on how strong our senses are. However, it's important to remember that just because we feel we may not have clear seeing as a strong sense, actually this sense – like every other – can be trained. We all have the ability to be psychic and to communicate with spirit, and whether we choose to do that within this lifetime is already written in our path. But I suspect that if you were not interested in psychism or already experiencing psychic sensations, you would most likely not be reading this right now.

Dreaming

Dreaming is a way in which our psychic senses and loved ones passed over, including spirit guides and higher angels, can get messages through to us, because we are in a more relaxed state of consciousness. So, I ask the question: if we all dream, then why do we NOT all believe that our dreams have particular meanings and messages? Maybe you have asked this same question?

Of course, not every dream is about being visited by a loved one we miss; lots of our dreams are a whole mishmash of different things we've been getting up to throughout our days and weeks. Yet not one person you ask will be able to deny that at some time they've had a strange dream of some sort that just felt so real or that has stuck with them.

Naturally, our dreams can also represent the darker side of the spirit world as well as the light, and these can scare us at times. It's important to access your dreams so you understand fully what the message is. You will remember I said that I was hungry to research and understand what exactly was going on for me with my clairs and spiritual senses, and my dreams played a big part in my research.

I would regularly Google the significant points that stuck with me after waking. For example, if there are animals, insects, birds, colours, symbols, locations, types of weather, people that you know, people that you don't know, they are all significant and our guides will be giving us these dreams to provide us with certain messages. The reason why it becomes all muddled up within the dream is because our brain is trying to make sense of it within the capacity that we use when in our waking life, yet when we are asleep our brain can access a much higher capacity.

I have learnt so much and added so much knowledge to my invisible spiritual dictionary from Googling the spiritual symbolism within so many dreams. And I know that this has been a huge factor in my awakening and understanding my spiritual journey.

Our dreams, as I said earlier, cover many aspects of our lives – past, present, and future – as well as people and situations, and not all dreams are loved ones visiting us. And although our dreams can determine how spiritually-minded we are, it doesn't mean that if you don't have spiritual dreams you are not spiritually-minded. You may be just more likely to have more visitations from loved ones passed over if you are working on your mediumship. In the same way, if you are really interested in past life regression and been working on that, you may well find yourself going to past lives within your dreams.

Our dreamlike state is the easiest way for our loved ones and spirit guides to get messages to us. The only downside is that we do not always remember our dreams, or may not realise that the dream was full of messages, so we are then left feeling like we had a bit of a strange dream – or even that we are a bit of a weirdo. How often have you have felt like that? In your waking life, you might be looking to understand what your senses are, yet it's also important to take into consideration that your dreams are adding to your evolvement and development within the psychic world.

Energy is everything. We are energy, and we drop into different levels of energy throughout our sleeping period. When we are more accepting of different densities of energy and understanding of our own energy levels, we will be more open to receiving guidance and also waking up our clairs and becoming more in tune with our spiritual abilities.

Let me tell you about a dream I had...

Not long after my beautiful grandmother, Meryl, passed over, my twin sister and I (we used to have a love/hate relationship) had a bit of a disagreement – one which had been going on for years, on and off. It felt for both of us like we were banging our heads against a brick wall with each other; we each had our individual views on the thing that we disagreed over., and we both felt trapped in a way, wanting the other to just understand.

One night, feeling stressed and just so stuck within this awful feeling, I went to bed and I had the most amazing dream. By this point, I was already pretty advanced with analysing my dreams, so I was able to understand the message when I awoke. As I slept, I was taken back to a time where my sister and I would sit on top of the garage roof in the warm sun, playing cards or playing with our toys together. I saw this memory as if I was really there within my dream; I could feel the warmth of the tin roof on my bum as I sat there.

We used to sit there with the kitchen door open, and could hear all the lovely sounds coming from inside our cosy home within. And this is what I was experiencing within this dream. I found myself jumping off the tin roof and going into the kitchen, making my way across the blue and white tiled floor, through the hallway and into our old lounge. My sister followed behind, and there standing in the lounge was my grandmother.

Now, I haven't been in this lounge since I was six years old, but as I said, it felt very much like how it used to. Grandmother didn't say anything to me and my sister, but just looked and smiled – and it felt SO GOOD. As she stood there, a huge white wolf came and stood beside her, staring at me and my sister. The wolf then continued to walk towards me and my sister, and stood in-between us.

In your dreams, you will know whether you are scared or not; it's all about the energy of what you feel in the moment. In my dream, neither my sister nor me flinched; we were not scared at all, and this wolf was not aggressive. Even though I was still asleep, I knew within this dream that Grandmother was letting me know that she was here to help me and my sister resolve our disagreement. I knew that she was watching over us, and knew exactly what had gone on and what was going to happen from then. I did not know what the wolf meant at that point, but I did know that the wolf was in some way bringing an extra message and helping.

Everything went hazy after that, and I came out of the

dream feeling a lot better. Later, when I was fully awake, I decided to research the spiritual symbolism of the wolf. I then went one step further and researched the symbolism of the white wolf, because I discovered that 'wolf' had an overall meaning, but each different coloured wolf had its own significance.

I found out that the white wolf meant a strong message from a spirit guide, and to help bring love and clarity back into a situation. Of course, it depends what you're using for your research and there are many different cultural symbolisms, but what I found really resonated with me at that time, and I have never forgotten the intensity of that dream. I felt comfort that my grandmother was completely supporting us with our disagreement, with no ego or judgment and no blame to either of us – just fully there, with pure love.

To some people, it could have seemed very strange seeing your grandmother standing staring at you beside a huge white wolf, but it helped me to move on from that disagreement with my sister and we finally let it go.

Our dreams can be such significant key healing points of our situations in life. So, it is really important to listen to them. Don't worry if you don't understand them yet. Just do the research on the symbolism, and you will better understand why you have them.

For me, that was a mediumship dream – a visitation from a loved one that I physically knew within this life. However, we can have other mediumship dreams where our ancestors, or other spirit who perhaps we didn't meet or know, visit us. And that can be more confusing for us. We will talk about that a little later.

Having a dream with no loved ones passed over and no visitation of some sort of spirit guide, is more of a psychism dream – within these dreams we can still receive messages and guidance for our life, etc., but the difference is that we do not feel or see any spirit. We may still experience colours, symbols, patterns, people, locations, types of weather, etc., and again we would need to research what each various point would mean.

Let me give you another example...

Years ago, I had a series of strange dreams that featured a particular woman or had the strong energy of the way she made me feel. This woman had been very mean to me when I was younger – or what I viewed to be mean – yet for some reason we seemed to be in each other's lives. I felt she was selfish and bullying towards me and it made me feel lacking in control. Eventually her behaviour became very reckless not just towards me but also to others, so I began to distance myself from her. But the dreams I had during that period were so intense and uncomfortable.

In one of the dreams, I found myself outside apparently enjoying a decent day in the countryside until suddenly a little dog started to attack me. I was trying to get it off me, but became aware within this dream that the little dog was fixated on biting my right hand. It particularly struck me that this specific area of my body was being attacked, and when I tried to get the dog away from me, it clung on and carried on biting my right-hand index finger.

When I woke up, I felt a little disturbed but yet again

decided to research the symbolism within this dream. I discovered that the right hand represented aggressiveness, authority, mercy, and power, and a dog biting your right hand signifies that someone has taken control of you and uses words to hurt you. Considering how I was affected by this woman's actions towards me, this all felt pretty significant.

I then found out that the right index finger represents your confidence, and again this made sense, because I had felt really low in confidence for a while around this particular lady. Even though I had distanced myself from her, obviously the situation and the energy involving the woman were still having an impact on me. And while I felt quite upset when I woke up, discovering the meaning fully by listening to this particular dream enabled me to ask for guidance and healing around the situation, through meditation and connecting with my guides.

You can again see how our dreams give deeper messages. This one in particular was focusing on a psychism energy. We must always watch and learn from the visuals in our dreams.

Dream Task

A simple little task, which you might have already done at some stage in your life, is to grab your special spiritual notepad and have it ready each night before you sleep, so that you can jot down what you experienced in your dream as soon as you wake up.

Make sure you write down:

What was happening in your dream.
How you felt within this dream.
Any people who were in the dream. Did you know them? How did they make you feel?
Were there any loved ones passed over visiting?
Any animals/birds or insects?
Any shapes?
Any patterns?
Any symbols?
Any significant colours that stood out?
Where were you in the dream?
What was the weather like?
What was the overall energy within the dream?

Once you have noted all of this down, Google the spiritual symbolism of the key things that stood out to you. Make sure you spend a bit of time checking a few different sites or looking up any symbolism books until you find the meanings, and you will definitely understand your dream much better. You will also know whether it was a psychic dream, a mediumship dream, or both.

Better yet, if you can do this more and more with each dream you remember, you will start to add to your own invisible spiritual book of knowledge. And even if you later forget the meaning of that dream, you will still have added to your evolvement in some way.

Out-of-body experiences (OBE)

Leading on from dreaming, another way of our internal

clear seeing will be out-of-body experiences. Some of you may have experienced this before, other may have done without realising it. The most common form of OBE will be when you fall asleep and then see yourself looking back at your sleeping body. You might see other aspects, too, like the surroundings. This happens in a submissive, subconscious way, where we have no control and can seem quite brief, which is often why people have no recollection of having an OBE.

On other occasions, you might remember, and this is an indication that your psychic energies have been working during your sleep. Whatever one sees within their OBE will be a spiritual psychic connection of some sort, which is why this is another form of clear seeing. We can also visit or see our loved ones who have passed over within an OBE, and again, this can be a very profound experience.

Let me tell you an interesting OBE of mine...

I attended The International Academy of Consciousness, where I trained in out-of-body experience and how to intentionally have one. As I explained earlier, the most common form will usually be during sleep, where we unintentionally have one. In this training, we learnt how to drop into a deep state of consciousness and deliberately leave our physical bodies. I managed to do this quite a lot, perhaps because I was already very in tune with my spiritual energy and doing very deep channellings which meant I was able to get out of my body quicker then others. But this does not mean that it cannot be achieved by any and everyone. As I said earlier, we are all energy, and we all have the ability to do all things psychic.

As I was in one of my particular OBEs, I experienced like a super sense, and it felt as though everything I saw and heard was heightened. Within this OBE, I saw many forms of energy that I might not usually be able to see in my physical form. I also saw my grandmother who had passed over, but she was chatting away to me.

I realised that me feeling drawn to do this training was to actually help me progress further as a medium and understand better what type of energy our loved ones are using when they come to connect with the living. The benefits of being able to do OBEs in a controlled manner are incredible, and bring much more awareness and clarity to each and every person within their own past, present, and future, and also bring much love, guidance, or closure on your loved ones. It also gives you the knowing that you can see your loved ones, and they are there.

The benefits of an uncontrolled OBE, such as one you just find yourself in, will be to bring more awareness to you of your psychic and mediumistic side. It will bring signals that your energy is shifting, or that you are receiving or strengthening your abilities, or that perhaps you need to listen to this clear seeing and start to focus your attention more upon your psychic side.

Meditation Visuals

Visuals during meditation is another form of clearseeing and will be an easier form of internally seeing for most, because many people practise meditation. Some visuals you receive during meditation may depend on what type of meditation you are doing, and whether you have an end goal or intention from that meditation. With that in mind, some people think or worry that they are making it up, especially if they wanted to focus on a particular relationship and then they see visuals of that person. Yet what you have to ask is: why did you feel drawn to focus on a particular topic with your meditation in the first place? It's because your intuition was being guided to what was needed for you at that time.

Within meditation, we can receive many different types of visuals and some people may have a great imagery focus, while others may not get much at all. But this does not mean that either is any less or any better than the other; it just highlights that possibly you do not have the internal clear seeing sensory working for you as strongly as other clairsenses, which you can most definitely choose to strengthen.

The internal visuals during meditation could include seeing a main colour, or seeing many colours, symbols or patterns, seeing faces appear or even visuals, as if you are watching a scene take place or possibly a memory-like feeling. Some describe it as watching a movie. Or you could be seeing various types of scenery, animals, locations, types of day, and weather. Whatever visual you see within a meditation is 100% correct for you to see at that exact time, even if you don't understand fully why. And that is why meditations are so beneficial for our spiritual development but also for our physical energy. When we are in a meditational state, we are more open to receiving the visuals that are being sent to us by our spirit guides or by loved ones that are communicating with us.

These visuals you see within your meditation will ignite other clairsenses that you have within your energy stream. So, depending on what you are seeing, it might ignite a certain sense of something or someone, or perhaps the visual will spark an emotional feeling within you which then kickstarts another visual. It's not uncommon during meditation to have certain physical feelings, too, and we will discuss this further in the clairempathy chapter.

It's important to know that not all meditation is gliding through a beautiful daisy field; sometimes we can get random visuals, or even ones that scare us, but this is ok. Your meditations are safe, and this could possibly just be indicating something within you that needs healing.

I have had so many intense meditations. One which I will never forget was where I found myself in a big house. There were parts of the outside of the building that looked like my Grandma's old house, and other parts that I had never seen before in this life, but I had the strong sense that I knew this house – so already my visual was kickstarting this sensing clair. As I walked into this house within this visual, I found myself in a room that didn't feel nice. I could see so clearly that the wallpaper was all dirty and peeling off, and the colours of the room were very bland. I felt a lot of sadness, fear, and anxiety when I first went into this room.

I then saw an old man standing at a grand piano, and it seemed silly that such a lovely piano was in this horrible, grim room. This old man freaked me out a bit, because he was acting crazily. He had a pipe hanging out of his mouth, but he was laughing, and his eyes were weirdly wide open. He was really into playing this piano, and very good at it.

He didn't say anything, but just carried on looking at me whilst playing this piano. Eventually I went out of that room and into another room on the right-hand side. It was a completely different type of room – tall ceilings, very grand, with lovely French furniture, nice big windows, very open and light. As I stood in this room, I looked out of the window and saw lovely, grand gardens, and off in the distance there was a man wearing an old-fashioned cricket outfit hitting a cricket ball in the field. As I watched this man, I was already aware of my sensory working, the feelings I got from this man, and who I felt he was.

Then I became aware of a woman standing behind me and I turned to see a beautiful lady around the age of 40, wearing a beautiful, black Victorian dress. It was buttoned up around the neck, and she wore a lovely pearl necklace around it. She was pretty, and her hair was very tightly pulled up into a neat bun, with slight curls around the front of her face. I could tell by the way she moved and dressed that she was very wealthy.

Once again, this ignited my senses and my clairempathy, and I felt really emotional: one, because I felt that even though she was very wealthy and beautiful, she was actually very sad within this stage of her life, and I felt she was really lonely; and two, because she made me feel loved and that she wanted to help me.

It took me six months to find out who she was, because in this vision no words were heard or spoken, so my clairaudient sense had not been ignited. As I came out of meditation, I had a strong sense of knowing that I had received something amazing and life-changing, even though I didn't fully understand yet. When I checked with my mum, she said that the way I described the house was just like my grandmother's house where she grew up. I had never seen or visited this house, but my mother showed me a picture and I was amazed to see that it was the exact house I had been seeing and had visited. My mum also told me that she thought the first man was my great-great-grandfather, because he smoked a pipe, had a grand piano, and was very eccentric. She didn't know who the lady was, nor the other man in the garden.

Within six months of having that particular meditation, and finding out who this lady was, my grandmother sadly passed over. So, one day while my mum was going through Grandma's boxes of old letters and photos, she sent me a picture she had found – and I was absolutely gobsmacked at what I saw. There was the lady, dressed in the exact clothing I had seen in that visual, her hair was the same, and the way she carried herself. I found out that her name was Emma Lena Burton, and she was my great-great-grandmother. I cried, because I finally realised why the vision felt so powerful and was so clear, and it was also amazing clarity to know that this lady I saw actually existed. We all question so much and we don't always trust, so we end up missing key connections or miss out on important messages that our loved ones try to show us.

We started to research our family tree, and I found out that the man I had seen in the garden was actually my great-great-grandfather, although I was seeing him as a younger version of himself. Sure enough, we found a photo of him in a newspaper wearing the cricket outfit which I'd seen in the meditation visuals. This particular meditation visual set in turn a huge amount of significant changes within my life, my family, my energy, and my own mediumship and psychic skillset. Ever since, I have been visiting them or had them visit me in dreams and meditations, and they now guide me.

I worked out that the left-hand room represented my past and my fears of what happened within my past, because every time I revisited that house, that left room became cleaner and nicer, and I felt less and less anxious. I started to understand that my great-great-grandfather came to me in that room to help me heal my past with men and from sexual abuse.

I found it so interesting to meet my ancestors after my grandma passed over, and it has since strengthened my communications with her. I realised that all my ancestors are guiding me and there was a bigger picture here for myself, for them, and for my family. So, that's how amazing visuals in meditations can be.

Of course, that was a very strong mediumship meditation, which at the time I had no clue I would venture into, but you can see by my example that you can experience such profound, life-changing visuals through your clear seeing sensory. This sense enabled me to move forward and understand my life, my future, and my roots, in a whole new way.

Not every visual in mediation is like this, and some people might not experience this intensity, but as I said it all depends on how aware of your clear seeing you already are and what your intentions are before you start meditating.

Meditation task

Make sure you have your notepad and pen to write down what you get.

Please note: do not do this technique if you are likely to be interrupted or distracted.

Begin by taking some deep breaths. On the third deep breath, hold this for the count of 3 (you will feel your head becoming lighter, and this is important because it helps you to drop into a deeper energy level. When you are in a deep energetic state, it becomes easier to receive many visuals.

As you exhale, take a fourth deep breath and count to 4, then as you exhale, imagine pure white, beautiful light cascading throughout your whole body until you are standing in nothing but the space of white light. It might even feel as though you don't have your body attached, but that is fine. Then just ask in your mind for your loved one or a spirit guide to start emerging from this light towards you, and see what you get and who you see. It may be someone you knew who has passed over and you recognise them, or someone who you don't recognise but you may sense that somehow you are linked, as in possible ancestors.

As you stand in the space of white light, just focus on the texture of their skin. Draw it in more and really focus on what you see, the shape of their face, the colour of their eyes. Are they smiling? Do they look serious?

It might even be a different type of guide, like an angel or ascended master who was never family. Just remember that whoever you see is completely right for you right now.

Just focusing on the visual, see if they are talking, or if they start to show you other visuals. Perhaps, if it's a loved one of yours, they might show you a memory of themselves or even a memory of you and them. Become aware of the other things that you feel when you see their face. Any feelings? Any emotions? Any physical sensations? Do you hear anything as you look at them?

You may call them in and only see a form of their body shape, or it might be very hazy – this is also ok. If it's your first time, you might need to practise more to strengthen the clear seeing sense within you, or it could be that they want you to understand something before they show more of themselves.

Make sure that you when you come out of this exercise, you ask the bright white light to become less and less, though still beautiful. Watch the light dim to a more natural level, then ask for protection and for you to be closed down enough to enable you to get on with the rest of your day in a practical manner.

Then immediately write down what you saw in as much details as possible, including your feelings and sensations.

This exercise is best to try on a day where you do not have too many things to do and don't need to go out, so I would recommend the evening time.

You will definitely find that by doing this technique even once, it will kick start your clear seeing. You may find that your psychic awareness feels stronger and that you start receiving more and more information psychically.

Visions

Now, visions are very similar to meditations, but they often come when we least expect them. So, this is a type of submissive clearseeing and one that we may not recognise happening to us and therefore miss the symbolism or messages.

We can see visions in our waking day-to-day life, whilst driving or out and about, and we can also have clear seeing visions just before sleep. The difference between visions in our waking life to visions during mediation is that they are often not as obvious or as clear to us. Visions can enter our mind at any given second, then trigger other clairsensory within our energy stream, so it's important to try to understand how our visions are working within us and how they THEN impact our feelings, thoughts, and emotions.

I would invite you to try to become more aware of the waking visions that you have. It is possible to be aware of them no matter how busy your mind or day. You can then begin to understand whether this vision is based on past, present, or future, and whether it's for you or a message about or for someone else.

Vision task (1)

Make sure you have a pen and pad.

Sit quietly.

Close your eyes.

Take a few deep breaths.

Without going into meditation, just ask in your mind to be shown something; absolutely anything.

Be open, with no expectation of what you will be shown.

Then watch this vision change and move. See how it forms. Does the vision look like just one image that stays the same and stays still?

Does the image have movement, or seem like you are watching a film?

Is the image clear or hazy?

Does the vision follow onto another part of imagery?

Is there anything in this vision that really stands out and keeps coming back or remains there throughout?

How does this vision make you feel? Are your other clairsenses being ignited, like feelings, thoughts, etc.

Do you know if this vision is about yourself? And if so, is it about your past, present, or future? Be really aware of what you are now thinking during this vision, or what it leads you to think.

Perhaps you now know this vision is not about you, but it's about someone else you know.

If so, become aware of why you are seeing this and what information or message you need to pass on.

If, for some reason, this visual makes you fearful – double check in your mind and ask: *Why am I feeling fearful? Is this really negative?* Or is it perhaps something that is just portraying a negative situation?

Take some deep breaths when ready, and open your eyes. Be prepared to write down everything that you saw, including what you felt or thought.

If there were any parts you didn't understand, Google the symbolism of the specific things in question. You will find that the spiritual meanings will very much fit in with your life or someone else's life.

Now, this exercise will be easier for some people than others because, as I explained earlier, some people are not very visual. However, when you practise these different visual techniques, your clear seeing will most definitely start to strengthen. Exercise two will be even more difficult for some.

Vision task (2)

Grab your pen and pad.

Sit quietly.

DO NOT SHUT YOUR EYES.

Take some deep breaths.

Stare at the same spot on your wall, or wherever you are looking.

Ask in your mind to be shown a visual with your eyes open.

No matter how strange it seems having your eyes open, stick with it.

You may feel resistant to this, as our natural desire would be to close our eyes to feel more relaxed. However, this will be key in training your clear seeing to become stronger and stronger.

Start to focus on any visual that comes to mind; if you feel you are distracted by what you were staring at, just go with it. Some of you may feel your eyes going fuzzy or hazy – that's brilliant. You might feel as though the wall you are staring at is moving or changing, even though its possibly a plain wall. That is normal, too.

Let your eyes be hazy. Not only does this focus on

your internal clear seeing, but it will also strengthen your external clear seeing (which we talk about in detail later).

See if you can focus on the visuals you receive; become aware of any significance in what you are seeing. Become aware of how you are feeling and what you are thinking.

Are you seeing as strongly as in the first exercise?

Ask the question in your mind: why do I feel this way, or why am I seeing this?

Perhaps you know again that this is about you or about someone else. Start to gather the information as to why you are seeing what you are seeing.

Take some deep breaths then bring your awareness back to the room.

Write down what happened and your feelings, thoughts.

REMEMBER

Compare both exercises.
Which exercise did you like best?
Why?
What did you struggle with?

REMEMBER

Google the symbolism of anything that stuck out for you within exercise two, for more clarification on what the meanings of your vision was.

As I said earlier, some of you will have found the first

exercise a lot easier, and please do not stress if you did, or if you felt you didn't receive a visual at all. This is all backed by energy and our clairs IGNITE other clairs, so even if you only saw a flash or a slight glimmer of something, that is enough to trigger more clairs. You will understand how this works the further we go through the different clairs.

TOP TIP

Once you have read every chapter on each individual clair, go back and try all the exercises again so that you have more awareness of the other clairs igniting through your clear seeing.

Premonitions and Déjà vu

Premonition Definition – A strong visual that alerts you to see something that is going to happen within the not-too-distant future. Can trigger you to feel certain emotions.

***Déjà vu* Definition** – French for 'already seen'

Well, well, well. Here, we are going to chat about premonitions – something which intrigues many people. Some people hear the word and totally freak, as there has often been a negative stigma attached to this word due to particular movies that focus on bad things happening.

That being said, premonitions can reveal both positive and negative things to come. Again, depending on whether you are following your spiritual development or not aware, may determine how you view a premonition if you have one.

Premonition can seem like *déjà vu*, but the difference between the two is really significant.

Firstly, premonitions tend to be stronger visions that are in more depth and which usually provide details of a not-too-distant future event. Usually, it's a bigger event in one's life, or even in the community or world.

Déjà vu involves less detailed and more hazy visuals about smaller aspects in one's future, and you can sometimes experience *déjà vu* years in advance of the actual real-life moment.

With both premonitions and *déjà vu*, we can never seem to pinpoint the actual moment we had the visual. We just KNOW we have seen it before.

Premonitions tend to bring on stronger emotions then *déjà vu* and this is usually because the premonition revolves around a bigger life event.

We all have the ability to see our futures, and when we have these visuals it's just our psyche tapping into parts of what's to come for us. Therefore, many believe that our lives are already written out for us.

Some claim that before we were born, we were given a contract to complete in each life, and when we become earth-bound it is then a part of our journey to unfold the lessons that we chose to learn in life. Some discover these easily, others have a hard time, but they believe it was written that way for some reason.

I had a hard time getting my head around this when I

thought of all the negative or awful things that happened to me in my past, but when I began to heal and unfold my true life purpose I really understood why certain things had happened and I started to believe in contracts of life.

It is not possible to bring on a premonition or *déjà vu*; they just happen. However, by training your clear seeing in different ways, it might help you to understand any premonitions that you do receive.

If you receive a premonition and you understand that's what it is, then you might well be able to prevent something or to change something slightly. Some people believe that if something is going to happen, then it WILL happen, and you can't change it – but YOU CAN be aware and prepared.

Premonitions usually happen during our waking life, and this is one of the only types of INTERNAL VISIONS that we are usually very aware of when it happens.

Premonition task

Grab your pen and pad.

Please sit quietly. and spend some time thinking about strong visuals you have had over the years that have really stuck with you.

Write down everything you saw and felt on those occasions.

Roughly how soon after your premonition did the incident happen?

This might be difficult for you if you experienced a negative premonition, so make sure you allow your emotions whilst writing this.

Be aware when writing that if it was a dream or in a meditation, this will not have been a premonition.

Please write down whether it was a premonition or *déjà vu*. Then, after reviewing it, do you now feel it was more of a *déjà vu*?

Déjà vu task

Grab your pen and pad.

Please sit quietly, and spend some time thinking of the times you have felt you had *déjà vu*.

Write down what happened and what the imagery was like.

Did you have any specific feelings then?

Could you recognise when you first had this *déjà vu*? (This is something that always intrigues people.) Even if you can't pinpoint the *déjà vu* visual actually occurring, can you get a sense of roughly how much time passed between first seeing it until the actual physical situation happening?

Please also write down if there have ever been times in your life where you have received *déjà vu* more than usual.

Then compare your notes with the premonition exercise, and make sure you fully understand whether this was a *déjà vu* or in fact a premonition.

Even if we go through stages where we receive more *déjà vu* than other times, it's simply our energy stream letting us know that we are on the right path and showing us small snippets of our future.

Sometimes the *déjà vu* visuals will be very boring, and

you will wonder why you are being shown that. Other times, it can be quite interesting and feel pretty significant.

Let me tell you about an experience I had with my déjà vu...

When I was about six years old, my mum took us on a little camping holiday. Whilst I was there, having fun running around in the early evening, I came across the main campfire. I suddenly thought in my mind that I had been there before. I recognised the big logs that were used as seats for people to sit on, and I was sure that I had already seen this exact thing at this exact moment in the day and had this exact feeling. I told my mum that I had been there before and had seen that campfire. Mum said, 'Honey, you have had *déjà vu*.' I wondered what on earth she was on about, but carried on running around playing. However, after years of learning my clairvoyance, I started to understand what had happened.

Yet what was interesting was that my mum had actually taken us on that holiday away from our home so my father could pack up his things and move out, without us being hurt. This *déjà vu* was the first one I remember and has always stayed with me, but I've since thought that I possibly had it because that holiday was going to mark a significant time to come regarding my father and my upbringing, where things changed dramatically.

I know this to be a *déjà vu,* because even though it was a clear visual, I still didn't see the actual event of my father leaving.

Let me tell you another déjà vu experience...

Another one that blew me away was when I was much older, around the age of twenty-six. I had been seeing my current partner for about three months when I stayed over his parents' house for the first time. We were just about to go to sleep, and he asked if I wanted a drink. As he left the room, I realised that I had already seen him leaving the room, the door closing, then me moving my eyes to the white wardrobe. I was seeing the exact same lighting within the room and at the same time of night. Yet this was my first time there.

I felt amazed when the *déjà vu* stopped and couldn't wait to tell him when he came back into the room. It felt so real and I had so much detail that I thought there must be something significant about our relationship. Little did I know then that I would go on to have my daughter with him and still be in this relationship now almost eight years on. So, again, with my hungry mind of always wanting to understand why I have certain visuals, it led me to believe that I was receiving another *déjà vu* that was leading or surrounding a significant time in my life where I would continue to be with this person.

These are two examples of *déjà vu* that I remember because they stood out. However, there will be ones where you don't really remember because perhaps they are just little glimpses that you're on track.

If you have *déjà vu,* you might question whether it means you're on the right track, especially if your life seems a mess. But REMEMBER your contract of life. There is always a reason for what's happening to you in your life.

Memories

Memories are very interesting indeed when they come into our internal clear seeing. We can experience memories of our own lives and we can also experience memories of spirit. When I'm doing readings for people, I often see memories starting to play out, like watching a movie in my mind. And I know that this is usually a memory that the sitter's loved one is giving to me. If the memory includes the sitter, it is obviously easier to detect that it's about them. But you could be shown a memory of your sitter's loved one passed over and does not include your sitter. Therefore, it's really important to watch carefully and begin to understand the feelings, thoughts, or sensations that are coming in and being ignited by this memory. That way, you can give a clear message about it. Memories are so important, as it could be this very memory that brings a transformation for yourself or for someone else.

We come across some difficulties if we are not a reader and just experiencing a memory of a spirit or of another person, and we find ourselves on our own when it happens. This means we are less likely to have confirmation straight away, so we might just shrug off the memory that we see. However, if we can train our clear seeing in focusing on strengthening memories, we will start to become more aware to take in the message of the memory and pass it on to whoever it is for.

If it's for ourselves, we will need to access the energy behind the memory to understand what the message is and why we are seeing this particular memory.

Memories can be presented very much like visions;

they can start and flash and then disappear, or they can remain and roll out like watching a movie. The memory may be hazy in areas, or very clear. The memory may merge into another memory from a completely different time in one's life, but for some reason you are seeing it this way. This could indicate that the two memories are connected in some way via energy.

Memories for ourselves can be tagged onto a vision, so you might be doing a meditation and just focusing on visualising, then you suddenly find yourself watching a memory. This is really normal, and it just means that the energy of the visualisation has brought you closer to this memory.

Memories from spirit are very interesting and can be very heart-warming, yet at times you could see memories of negative experiences which the spirit went through. So, it's important to really be aware of what your body is doing and what other clairs are being ignited within you as a result of this memory. Do you feel suddenly very sad or anxious? Or perhaps you feel overwhelming love. These feelings are the clairemotional triggering from this memory, and will help you to better understand the message or the spirit that is communicating with you and what they are wanting to say.

Memories can also be shown to you in your dreams, OBEs, and meditations, as well as in your mind's eye – all of these, as explained within this chapter, are part of your clear seeing. You cannot experience a memory without clairvoyance. So, for those of you who say you are not clairvoyant: think again, lovely person, because you ARE. Every single person has a memory at some point, just like every single person has a dream at some point, even if you can't remember it.

Sometimes people may see the same memory coming to them over a period of time, and this can represent that there is clearing needing to take place, possibly around what the memory holds or the people within the memory. If it goes hazy, it could represent that you have blocked something from this experience, and it's gone into a deeper subconsciousness within you that will be impacting your life on some level.

Memory exercise

Grab your pen and pad.

Sit quietly.

Close your eyes.

Take some deep breaths.

With the intention in your mind, ask to be shown a memory – any memory that needs to be shown.

Watch how it comes in, and how it unfolds.

Notice whether it merges into different memories, and whether it's hazy in some places or clear.

Then become aware of how this memory makes you feel and the thoughts now running through your mind. Don't push out any thoughts, even if they seem random, or if it's about someone or something from a long time ago. This will be important.

You may not understand straight away, or you may feel like asking for guidance as to why you are seeing this memory.

Come out of memory and write down all of the above in your special notepad.

TOP TIP

Do this in the evening, or on a day where you are not very busy and will not be distracted, as it may make you feel very emotional. Be prepared to take on the memory if you feel it's something that is representing a blockage, and KNOW that healing will be on its way for you, or seek next steps to help unblock whatever has come up.

Memories and past lives

This is interesting, as often people find themselves having visuals that they feel they recognise and know, as if it should be a memory of theirs, but they also know some things look different. I have had some profound amazing past life memories that played out for many years but became stronger and stronger at certain periods of time. You would need to go into a past life regression to be able to connect fully and understand this, and to heal it, if that is needed.

Flashbacks

Flashbacks are very similar to memories, but the difference is that flashbacks are short, fast visuals of a memory. Usually flashbacks can seem more intense and we can see them in our waking life. The reason for flashbacks will be to alert us of something that we need to remember, which will then lead to clearing or healing – and this can be positive or negative. Flashbacks are another form of clear seeing, but they can trigger our other clairs to ignite, therefore bringing us certain feelings, thoughts, sensations, etc. So we must listen and feel those sensations to understand what the message is for us.

It is most common within our own selves to receive a flashback; we do not very often receive flashbacks of spirit or other people. So this is more of a personal experience.

Flashbacks within our past lives can happen, too, and will play out in a similar way as described earlier. We will feel as though we know or have seen that flashback before, wile knowing that the time period or life is different.

When you do your memory exercise, think about whether it feels more like a flashback or a memory, and see if you can start to understand fully the difference between flashbacks and memories.

Colours inside the mind

Colours are so amazing. They can tell us so much about what we need at a particular time in our life, as well as connecting to spirit. They can represent so many powerful messages. A lot of people are able to pick up on colours in their mind's eye quite easily, and I've noticed through teaching many students that those who struggled to visualise were still able to at least see colours within their mind. Colours can come into meditations, and we can see whatever colours are correct for us at that time. Or if we are guided to think of a particular colour, then our minds will focus on that.

Colours trigger our other clairsenses because they make us feel certain things. We might also have personal attachments to particular colours, so we can even become very overwhelmed or emotional when seeing them. Likewise, there are some colours that we might find displeasing, or even scary and disturbing.

Colours hold energy, and they can lead us to understand possible blocks in our body or life, or can lead to memories, thoughts and feelings. So, colours can trigger other clear seeing to set in, like memories and visions.

For example, if you have a lovely, vibrant, bright, sunshine yellow that would make you feel very warm and happy, it might also remind you of a nice experience you had or of a particular person. However, if you saw this sunshine yellow and it was hazy or more cloudy-looking, it could indicate that you not feeling so happy and positive.

Likewise, a bright red might make you feel love or passion if it's a nice rosy red, or it could make you think about your willpower; if it's more of a bright, angry red, this could make you feel angry and annoyed. Again, the colour red could represent physical or emotional wounds. If the red colour is sluggish or cloudy, this could represent that you're feeling unloved or that you are missing something in these areas. There are so many meanings and reasons why we see colours and what each shade means.

Again, you may see colours within dreams, memories, meditations, visions, or *déjà vu*. Colours are absolutely everywhere.

You could find yourself sitting in a meditation and just experiencing different colours over and over, or witnessing the same colour merging into different shades of itself.

Colour exercise: One

Grab your pen and pad.

Sit quietly.

Close your eyes.

Take some deep breaths.

Start to THINK about the colour red and focus specifically on that colour. Perhaps you start to see the red coming into your mind's eye. As you focus on this red, begin to change the colour within your mind to an ORANGE colour, and continue to focus now on what shade of orange you are seeing.

Watch how the colours merge into each other. Become aware of how these particular colours make you feel. What do you think of when you see these colours?

Ask yourself these questions:

1. Is it hard to focus on the same colour?
2. Can you see the colour you requested clearly, or is it hazy?
3. Did you see it at all? Don't worry if you didn't, because you will still have other clairs working within you.

Write down what you experienced. Then go into the exercise again, and this time add in more colours. Be open to whatever colours are coming in one after another; see how they merge, and how they appear to you.

Be really present to what you feel. YES, YOUR MIND MAY WANDER – but ask yourself WHY? Perhaps these colours are making you think about something important in your life?

Colours bring up so much emotion within us, and it's important to be aware of this. We can detect positive and negative feelings and messages by the colours that we see and feel.

Colour Technique: Two – Mediumship and Colour

Sit or lie down comfortably.

Close your eyes.

Take some deep breaths.

With each breath, count to three before exhaling, and start to welcome the pure white light into your energy stream. As you focus on this white light, practise drawing this white light in stronger.

When you feel the energy of this white light, or it looks very bright, ask to receive a colour from a loved one in spirit, and watch or feel this colour starting to come in.

Access how it comes in – does it overflow?

Does it present itself as a flash of colour?

Does it shine like a ray of light?

Does the colour persist, or go quickly?

Does the colour start to merge into another shade or a different colour?

As you are receiving this colour, access how you feel. What emotions are you experiencing? What are you thinking?

Who are you thinking of or aware of in spirit? Perhaps you already knew straight away which loved one this is. Perhaps you're not sure and that is fine. Maybe this colour reminds you of this loved one. Perhaps this colour was their favourite colour, or is somehow linked to something that was important to them.

Once you have watched this colour and you are aware of spirit, you can take this technique further by asking if there is a message from them. Then see what you feel, think, or see.

Take a nice deep breath and bring yourself fully out of the technique, opening your eyes when ready.

TOP TIP ONE

When focusing on mediumship techniques and drawing the white light in strongly, it can make us feel lightheaded afterwards, so make sure you do grounding and protection.

TOP TIP TWO

I would also advise you to do this particular technique when you don't have a really busy day. It can bring up emotions within you if you are visited by a loved one that you miss, so you will need time afterwards to access your emotions.

Shapes and patterns

Shapes also play a key part in our internal clear seeing. They often appear during meditations and dreams, but can also appear in different forms of visions. They are very interesting because we might not have seen a particular shape before yet when we do see it, we know it has a meaning of some sort. Then we just have to try and get to the bottom of it.

Let me tell you about an experience I had when I kept seeing a triangle. It was when I first decided to actively develop spiritually. Each week, the teacher would do a meditation and I would find that I kept seeing a triangle. I was curious why, and did not understand straight away. However, I would find myself wanting to put my fingers together, and I realised whilst in meditation I was creating the downwards triangle I was seeing in my visions. It felt good to do this physically.

I noticed that I was always drawn to making this triangle with my fingers then holding it near my womb area. If I moved my hands, it didn't feel right, and the pull to have it by my womb was so strong. I started doing this more and more in my day-to-day life, and I just knew that there was something very significant about this symbol and for me to see it and then create it with my hands.

A lot of people know that the downward triangle represents one of the spiritual elements, which is water. So, I found this interesting, because I have always been drawn to water and love being in water whenever I can. However, when I finally decided to Google the symbolism of making that symbol with my hands, I was excited to find images of women all over the world making that same pattern with their hands, and over many generations, from witches and goddesses to women in government. Maybe some of those women didn't realise what they were doing, but I also knew that some were deliberately making that symbol. When I saw these pictures and read the articles, it gave me so much clarity as to why I was being shown it to start with. It is a highly feminine symbol for women, using their womb power to create what they want through the greater good and for the better of mankind.

I now use this symbol on a daily basis in my meditations, classes, and on my social media images, as well as on my website. Have a deeper look and you will see them.

Shapes exercise

Grab your pen and pad.

Sit quietly.

Take some deep breaths in.

Begin to immerse yourself in pure white light and start to focus on a shape that you know, like a square. Keep focusing on this square, making sure you are fully thinking or seeing it. Practise visualising the sides of the square, making sure you can see the whole shape.

Become aware whether it's clear or hazy. Perhaps you get flashes of this image, or maybe you hold it for a long time in your mind's eye.

Now, focusing on that clair, practise watching the square turn into a 3D version, and watch then how the lines form and change, feel how it changes shape and perhaps becomes bigger or smaller. As you practise this, be aware of whether there are any colours to the lines or around the shape.

Is it still in pure white light? Or a different colour now? Immerse yourself in the amazingness of how you can draw this into your mind's eye and play with it.

Now change the shape into a triangle and see how it merges and forms. Do you still see the square? Or does it change easily? Again, is it hazy or clear, does it last long or are there just short glimpses? There is no right or wrong; it's just experimenting.

You can either continue to go through different shapes, or take some deep breaths and come out of the exercise.

Make sure you write down exactly what you saw and how it played out.

Did you find this easy or difficult?

TOP TIP

Remember you are focusing on the shape you are requesting, so you must be a little strict about how you focus on the technique, but be open when you invite the shape to merge and change.

Shapes Exercise: Two – Being open with shapes

This particular technique is more open, so you can be less restricted with how you work it.

Grab your pen and pad.

Sit quietly.

Close your eyes and begin to take deep breaths.

When you are nicely relaxed, ask to be given a shape or a pattern in your mind's eye. Allow whatever shape or pattern in, even if you have never seen it before. Watch or feel how this shape moves and looks.

Become aware of the colour of the shape/pattern, and observe how it changes. Again, note whether you are seeing it in short flashes, or if the visual stays very clear within your mind's eye.

Become aware of how this shape triggers your other clairs, and what you are feeling or thinking. Perhaps you feel certain emotions when seeing this shape, or you are drawn to a particular country or a period in history.

Maybe you are aware of a loved one or a high spirit guide giving you this shape, and it relates to them. Consider that this shape could maybe even represent a past life of yours, and that it's important as to why you are now receiving it.

You can then come out of the exercise and write down everything you experienced and in what order it triggered your other senses.

TOP TIP

It's important to document your spiritual findings and experiences. It allows you to go back and look at what you received, as what you experience could be ongoing and will present more pieces to a puzzle that you are meant to understand. Looking back will help you to understand the full picture over a period of time.

Auras within your mind's eye

Auras are amazing things. The most common way of seeing auras will be internally, with your eyes shut. However, some people can see auras of others with their eyes open. This may come naturally or within in time, after practising.

We can view auras of humans, animals, plants, and objects. Spirit, however, do not hold an aura, because they no longer have a physical body. That is why usually when we feel or see spirit, we see either white light, gold or, if more of a negative spirit, we may even see grey or black.

Auras are very important, as they will tell us a lot about each other, and will change over time depending on what a person is going through. Auras can also show emotional and physical blockages from previous trauma.

Our auras can have gaps and holes, so sometimes we may see more than one colour, then the colour can look or seem hazy, or we may even see the holes.

Because colours have meanings, we read the aura based on either what each colour means, or what we perceive that colour to mean by how we feel about that colour.

Our aura is an energy field we hold around us, and people can tell how we feel because our auras hold the energy and emotions.

Aura Exercise

Grab your pen and pad.

Sit with another person.

Look at this person with your eyes open, then close

your eyes and imagine you can see the outline of their body. As you do this, you will start to see that the outline has a colour, so focus on that colour and allow your mind to show you a bubble of colour around the person. Be aware of the most prominent colour.

Ask in your mind what this colour means for this person and listen to your mind. Trust in what you feel or think.

Ask your mind whether you feel this colour is relating to their emotions or if it's a physical issue that they have going on.

See whether you feel there are merges in colour and whereabouts on the body they are.

Access whether the colours are very bright, or if they are sluggish and hazy – this will help you to access whether there is something negative going on for them in the area of what this colour means.

See if you notice any holes or gaps within the colours as well.

Be aware whether you feel any physical sensations within your own body suddenly, and know that this is most likely something this person experiences in their own body.

Open your eyes and tell this person what you saw and what you felt each colour means for them. Don't worry if you're not sure what each colour means; just trust your instinct on it. Then let the person clarify what's correct.

TOP TIP ONE

Be very open to whatever you receive. Don't get hung up on worrying about the meaning of the colour, as lots of websites will give different meanings to colours. Trust your intuition and go with what you FEEL the colour means for that person.

REMEMBER

Your first thoughts are key. Because they are usually 99% correct.

TOP TIP TWO

When working with other people, they may be fixated on an answer for themselves so may overlook what you say. Make sure you make them aware to be very open to whatever you say and see. Also guide them into looking outside the box, and give them pointers to their past, present, or future thoughts, as a lot of people will overlook or forget past events, yet we still hold them within our energies. So, if something is unresolved, our auras will show this.

TOP TIP THREE

If you see lots of grey or dark colours around the other person, don't go overboard with how you tell them this, because it could upset them. Again, it's important to consider how you relay information to others, because dark colours can represent depression, difficulties, heavy energy, tiredness, or blockages that are set quite deep within us. So please do scare them, always be kind and compassionate when presenting the information

TOP TIP FOUR

If you have picked up something negative and you tell the person, please be aware that they might not want to disclose certain information so you may not get full clarification. This can be frustrating, but we must be respectful of people's emotions and energy.

Chapter 3

Clairvoyance – External Clear Seeing

Now that we have discussed in depth the internal clear seeing aspects of Clairvoyance, I would like to chat to you about our external clear seeing.

External clear seeing simply means seeing outside of our body, not in our mind's eye. This can include seeing energy within the atmosphere, shadows, flashes of light, orbs, auras, and spirit.

Many people feel concerned at the thought of external clear seeing, because they instantly think they will be seeing ghosts walking around left, right, and centre. If you're like me, and strong with your senses, then yes, you might very well see them daily from all angles, but this is not the case for the majority of people.

We all use our external clear seeing on a daily basis, and the things we view or see are then soaked into our consciousness where we perceive them in our own way. For instance, someone who is colour blind will view the colour red differently to someone who is not colour blind.

Or if we are sitting on a bench people-watching, each person watching will view the same person differently, based upon what we see first. Then, what we externally see triggers what we THINK or FEEL. These are all forms of our clairsenses kicking in, but those who are not aware of that will just assume it's their thoughts. Although these situations and reactions are normal, we must become aware of how we PERCEIVE, and if we JUDGE.

The reason we discuss external clear seeing and why it is an important sensory is because we will see things that make us question ourselves. They can seem strange and not feel like the usual things we see. We can clearly explain seeing a person who is alive smiling at us, or seeing a picture in a book, but we cannot always explain seeing a flash of white light spin past us when were in bed and all the lights are off. Again, this more unusual external clear seeing will trigger emotions, thoughts, feelings, etc, within us. We might suddenly on edge or scared, or maybe we feel overwhelming love. We might suddenly feel freezing cold or even nice and warm.

We will discuss in detail how to determine the difference between knowing what's positive and negative with regards to the things we externally see.

External Seeing

This includes every type of seeing outside of your physical form.

Here's a reminder of what this may include:

Seeing spirit within our outside surroundings.
Seeing objects moving around.
Seeing shadows.

Seeing flashes of light.
Seeing orbs.
Seeing energy within the atmosphere.
Seeing auras of people/animals/plants/objects with your eyes open.

Externally Seeing Spirit

This is one of my personal favourites, and I have had a huge journey with externally seeing spirit. I have been through some very scary externals and some also amazing life-changing ones. I understand the journey is very confusing at times and it's one I have never forgotten. I used to question why I was seeing a whole mixture of things – sometimes for long periods of time, other times it would die down for a while.

I would find myself feeling very drained at stages and I was more fearful of that than actually externally seeing spirit. I would often question whether my mind was playing tricks on me. Did I really just see something or someone moving around? At times, I even questioned my mental state.

You see, I started to see spirit externally wandering around when I was very young; my earliest memories are when I was four years old. However, I did not realise at that time that they were spirit.

Babies and children will often see spirit outside of the mind, because they are still very innocent and spiritually open. What makes us lose that sense is related to how we grow up and become socially conditioned. Our cultures and the religion/beliefs that we hold also have a strong impact on our views regarding spirit. However, we will still receive spiritual visions and messages, yet just not realise it.

I was fortunate to be brought up believing in spirituality and being supported by my mother and I feel this helped me a lot to understand my senses. But it can be a strong block for some people if they feel their friends and family do not believe in spiritual things.

You see, the energy is always there, whether we are spiritual or not.

Let me share one of my experiences that scared me to begin with...

When I was in my early to mid-twenties, spirit became quite rife in showing themselves to me often, and at times I questioned whether I was actually insane. I went through a bad period within my life, where I took a lot of drugs and my senses became enhanced, and when you intoxicate yourself you wonder if it's the drugs or whether you really are seeing things walking around that look or seem not of this dimension. Unfortunately, my drug-taking continued on for many years and I went down a slippery slope in self-destruct mode, which felt very dark. So, the things I externally saw began to look and feel of a darker nature, which made me anxious, agitated, and scared. Again, though, it was hard to determine if it was as a result of the drugs or my spirituality.

Finally, I managed to find a light at the end of the tunnel, and I started to recover from my drug addiction, eventually becoming clean from drugs. This process was truly amazing, but it was also the hardest time in my life, because I found that I had nothing – apart from trusting in the light I always saw to guide me.

When I became clean, I realised that these strong senses were still there. These external visuals were still really prominent in my life and I was still experiencing spirit visiting. Sometimes I would see light figures, other times I would see dark figures; some moved quickly, some moved very slowly; some flashed, and some looked sludgy. And as I was then clean from drugs and sober, I began to realise that it was not the drugs

I would get such a clear glimpse of their faces on some occasions, and at other times would just see their outline. But as time went on, I began to understand the difference between dark spirits and light spirits, and while I still often felt fearful, the more this happened the more I started to understand protection.

Eventually, I went to a lady to have a spiritual clearing, and she trained me in protection and how to control what was coming to me. At the time, I did not want this sense, because it was too intrusive in my life. I just wanted to be a photographer and get on with a quieter life, yet my trainers told me over and over that I would be a medium one day. I was adamant that they were wrong, because I saw this sense as something that scared me. I did not want to communicate with spirit because it drained me, and I was always shocked to see them wandering around my room – even if they were nice spirits. I just didn't want it.

Little did I know that two years later I would become a medium, create a successful business, and teach others how to become mediums. For someone so psychic, my guides well and truly kept that part of my life quiet.

External Clear Seeing Exercise

I would like you to focus on a time in your life when you feel you saw a spiritual experience with your eyes open. Get your notepad and write the answers down to the questions below:

1. Where were you when you saw something in your surroundings?
2. How did the spirit present themselves?
3. Were they clear, were they hazy, was it fast or slow when it happened? Did you see features or just an outline of them?
4. How did this make you feel?
5. Were you feeling love and comfort? Or did you feel scared and unsafe?
6. Were you able to understand who they were? Perhaps a loved one? Or perhaps a spirit you do not know, just wandering about?
7. Be really aware of this memory and make sure you are focusing on a time when you definitely feel that you saw something *outside* of your mind – because remember, we have internal clear seeing which involves the things inside our mind.
8. Make sure you are accessing exactly the clairs that were being ignited when you saw this, and that you're not getting it mixed up.

Let me tell you a story of when I saw a darker spirit...

It was about a year after becoming clean, and I was living in my new home. Unfortunately, because of the drug-taking, even though I was sober I still often experienced nightmares. Through intoxicating myself, I had opened up gaps and holes within my auric energy field, so spirit were quite easily able to get in and reside within my energy. This was all before I had that clearing I spoke of earlier, and before I had even thought of becoming a medium.

One night, I was lying in bed on my own in the dark. I had been awake for a while from a nasty nightmare, and I felt uneasy. I heard my bedroom door open. When I looked, I saw that my door was actually physically opening, then I saw a dark shadow run through my bedroom from the door and actually pounce on my bed towards me. I was able to put my hand up and say 'NO!', which made the shadow spirit back off. But it didn't go.

I knew by the feeling, not by the sight, that it was a male spirit. He then stood at the end of my bed. I knew that he was waiting for me to sleep so that he could try to do whatever he wanted to do. Often, it's just to feed off your energy, which makes you incredibly drained.

I then started to call upon my spirit guides and the pure white light that I trust in so much, because I knew he was not going. Eventually, the white light became so strong for him that he had to leave. So, the white light I saw was internally in my mind, but it was still so strong to make him externally leave.

The way he jumped onto the bed was like a pouncing

jaguar, and I saw that with my eyes open. The feeling I got was not nice and he felt quite predatory. I knew enough by then to know the types of entities that are around, and I would experience things like this very often. Obviously, now I don't receive darker energies as often, because I have learnt sufficient grounding and protection techniques needed to keep me safe.

Now let me tell you of a time I saw light spirit...

Gosh, where do I start? I have so many external clear seeing experiences I want to tell you about (maybe I will write another book just for all of them!). This particular experience, though, was extremely profound and life-changing for me.

When I was twenty-six, I found myself in my little flat, in my new world of being sober. It was still very early days and an awfully difficult time. I felt very lonely and as if I had literally nothing left in my life. Those days were agonising and uncomfortable and I struggled not to go back to my old ways and intoxicate myself. I would spend the day on my own in my little flat, crying all day, and playing with the knife that seemed to offer me a way out of my pain. It was as if I had a split personality: one minute I would be feeling very sorry for myself; the next minute I would hate myself and have so much anger about everything I had done and what I had become.

On one such day, I eventually went to sleep. When I woke up, I saw a figure sitting on my bed. This being was the purest white I had ever seen, so glowing and beautiful, and instantly made me feel safe and calm. I took a while to get my thoughts together as I was unsure if I was dreaming. But no, she stayed there, and I started to realise it was my mum's best friend, Mellie, who I would often call to – in my mind – for help, especially when I was getting clean. In my fucked-up state, crying, I had often desperately asked her to just show me a sign. Well, she was most definitely giving me a sign by sitting on my bed!

There is no way I imagined it, because the visual resided outside of my mind for so long, or at least it felt for long. Afterwards, I felt something had been lifted, and I could not stop thinking about the way she had smiled at me.

From then, things started to slowly but surely change. And that is when I began to understand my senses more deeply, but also part of my purpose path. I started to open up again to spirituality and found that I was able to start working on healing my heart from my pain and past actions. The huge healing journey would prove to be a three-year process, but that was the start of it and the reason why it's one external visual I will never forget. I know now that it was meant to be so astounding to keep me going.

Have you ever experienced anything like this? Go back to the external clear seeing task I set earlier, and go through the questions again. Or perhaps you have now remembered another time that you want to write down. If you make a note of what you experience, it can really improve your senses and is a handy reference for the future.

Of course, we can be scared of seeing spirit in our physical surroundings, but we should remember that spirit resides everywhere, and we are not alone. Spirit is a form of energy, and energy is everywhere and everything. So, to me, it's so normal for spirit to show themselves externally. And the more you develop your senses, the less scared or shocked you will become.

When I see spirit externally now, whether light or dark, I'm like, '*OH, HEY THERE, YOU'VE POPPED IN TO SAY HELLO.*' Or if it's dark, I'm like, '*OK, LET'S GET YOU GONE*' – in a nice way. Because even dark spirits have light within them; they have just lost their way and need guiding back to their true path. Sure, some of them will pipe up and make it difficult, and some may not actually be as bad as you think. They deserve a chance to go home to the light, just like all of us.

Peripheral vision

Definition: A vision as it occurs outside the point of fixation, i.e. away from the centre of gaze. The vast majority of the area in the visual field is included in the notion of peripheral vision.

Have you ever found yourself minding your own business and then, out of nowhere, you see something walk past out of the corner of your eye? You find yourself questioning whether someone just stood there? Well, my friends, that's because you *did* see something.

We often question when this happens, and we usually offer ourselves the explanation that we've been imagining it or we're just tired. But really, we need to understand that this area of our external vision is wide open and has been untrained through life. If you think about it, all our life we are programmed to see shape, form, and structure. We are also programmed to see things that we are told are normal. Spirit and energy, or that of the unexplained, are still not considered normal in this day and age. On top of that, if we are brought up in a family of non-believers, this will also have an impact on how we view peripheral vision.

Our vision from the corner of our eye can be trained, just like our frontal vision. The more we train our external clairvoyance, the more we can see spirit and energy with our eyes open, and the more centred our frontal vision will become.

So, next time you have those images that make you question if someone just walked past you, you know now that there was most likely 99% someone in spirit there.

Seeing objects moving

As with seeing spirit externally, we can also see *things* moving externally outside of our mind's eye – this will usually be because of spirit. So, although we might not see the actual spirit, we might see objects and items being moved around. This could be very sudden or very slow. Again, if we are not used to this type of thing, we can find ourselves questioning whether it really moved, or if we are going a bit crazy.

How objects move and why, will be down to the type of spirit that is moving them and what type of environment they reside in. Some movement could be in a nice way, for the spirit to simply show a loved one that they are around. Or it could be in more of an angry manner, possibly to torment the living, for whatever reason.

How you would determine the movement also depends on how the movement happens and how it makes you feel, or the energy you feel before and after the movement. So, it's very important to access this feeling. However, if you feel in danger or scared, you must get a professional medium to give you advice on the best way to sort it out.

Seeing shadows

Seeing shadows is something that many question. Is this normal? Am I just imagining this? And sometimes when we see shadows, it can be quite scary, but you might remember when I mentioned about the energy before and after seeing the shadow. It's all about how the shadow occurs as to whether you should be scared of it.

The important thing to consider is:

1. Where are you seeing this shadow?
2. Does it happen at similar times of day or night?
3. How do you feel when you see this shadow?

Perhaps you remember a time when you saw shadows of the unexplained nature, and these questions make you think back to when you did experience this.

We can also see shadows when lying in bed in the dark, which can feel really strange and we are unsure whether it's just the darkness. But we must not ignore the ENERGY.

It's important to remember that not all shadows are of a darker nature or negative. Not all shadows are black, either; we can see all sorts of shadow colours and forms.

However, if you are receiving shadows just before nightmares or after nightmares, I would seek a professional medium's advice.

TOP TIP

We also have shadow sides of ourselves, so sometimes when shadows present themselves, it's really important to access what's going on within your mind and body to try and understand your own shadow self.

You will usually see shadows as an external clear seeing. However, some forms of shadows can occur in visions and dreaming, which are an internal clear seeing.

Seeing flashes of light

Flashes of light are exciting to see externally, and can often be very positive signs for you. However, some people still get scared of this as it can feel shocking or unexplained.

When I would be going through deep spiritual upgrades, I would often get flashes of light with my eyes wide open. It would happen so strongly that it would make me jump, but I never felt unsafe. It made me feel excited, because I saw it as a sign that something spiritually had evolved within me. The flashes of light would start as small white bolts of light, then over the years developed into larger bolts of white light, until eventually I would see electric blue flashes of light, too.

I have found that these flashes don't happen all the time, but when they do, you will be going through a spiritual process, or it will be a sign from a loved one or your angel that they are helping you with something.

White light exercise

Think back to any times where you have seen flashing bolts of light?

What colour was it?

When did the flash of light occur?

How did it make you feel?

Can you remember what you were going through in your life when this happened?

Write it all down, as this will help you to remember when and exactly why this happened.

TOP TIP

Always make sure you write things down then go back over them. When you access why and when things are happening, you might notice a pattern. It's our responsibility to be aware and start understanding why certain things are happening.

Seeing orbs

Orbs are so interesting, even though some people put orbs down to particles of dust. Yet when you watch videos of dust movement and orbs moving, you can see a clear difference. Some orbs are also different colours, not just white, so we need to take this into consideration when we think they are dust.

Some people can see external orbs, and they will usually be presented in the external clear seeing. We rarely see orbs within our internal clear seeing.

I have one student who sees orbs regularly, and this is a way in which she detects that loved ones are around. It comes naturally to her and seems to be her strongest sense, and from this she can then use her other clairs to help her to understand details of who this orb is.

Orbs are usually loved ones passed over, or even spirit stuck within buildings or environments. So some people might see orbs in an old pub or haunted house, or perhaps even in an ancient land.

Orbs can present themselves in different sizes, but are often of a rounded shape. We must make sure we know the difference between a flash of light and an orb, but they will both be forms of identifying spirit.

Orbs, as explained earlier, will sometimes present themselves in different colours, and again it's down to you to detect why it's a different colour.

There have not been many cases of dark coloured orbs, which suggests that orbs are usually positive spirit with good intentions.

This student I mentioned earlier feels the energy of orbs

and believes that you can draw them in even more. Her nan, who she was really close to, passed away. About one week after she had passed over, this girl went to her nan's house on her own, and set her phone onto video mode. Then she began to sing *Amazing Grace*, as she had always promised her nan that she would sing this song to her after she passed.

When she began to sing, you can see on the video that the orbs start to appear more and more, and in all different shapes and sizes. You can feel the energy through the video.

Some people might not have seen that whilst in the room and could only see it through the video. But because my student can externally see orbs, she wanted to see if she could make them move more. By singing and keeping a promise, she got the orbs to react.

Orb exercise

Get your notepad and write down the answers to these questions:

1. Have you seen orbs with your eyes open?
2. If so, how did you feel?
3. Did you know who the orbs were when you saw them?
4. Were they fast moving or slow moving?
5. What colour were they, and what size?

TOP TIP

If you are someone who sees orbs a lot, why not see if you can take a video and sing or play music in an environment which once belonged to the person you want to contact? If you can no longer use their environment, perhaps find an item that once belonged to them and try to video that whilst singing or playing their favourite song, and see what happens.

Orbs represent animals and plants/trees, too.

Let me tell you about a time when I was younger...

On one occasion, I had visited my dad and was sleeping in his spare room. There was a house plant on the desk by the wall. When I was trying to sleep one night, I became aware that out of the darkness I could see this little orb moving around. I had to shake my head because I thought at first I was imagining it. However, it didn't go away so I started to wonder what it could be.

It was only hovering around the plant – nowhere else – but I could clearly see that this white ball was moving around. At that time, I liked to think it was a little fairy. My parents had always been open about spiritual things and magical aspects, so I wasn't scared. Also, I was picking up on a happy, positive energy. Eventually, I fell asleep.

The next morning, I got up and went straight to the plant, and noticed there was a little white feather. Now I didn't know at that time that white feathers meant that a loved one had visited, but the white feather did draw me in and got my attention, which is exactly what your loved ones want if they are sending you a sign.

I rang my mum and she said that the ball of light would

have been the energy or spirit of the plant, because plants are living things and hold energy as well. She then told me the feather was a recognition that my loved ones knew I had seen the plant orb, so I'd had two visits – one from the plant, and one from a loved one.

I never forgot that experience and it still feels really clear, even to this day.

There have also been other interesting topics on orbs connected with extra-terrestrial beings (ETs) or aliens, should we say.

Let me tell you another awesome experience...

My family have always been interested in visiting crop circles that have been created in the fields, and we specifically like going to Avebury where there are many crop circles and sightings. This is very close to Stonehenge, so the energy is really magical in all these surrounding areas. We go every year, and no matter whether the crop circles are man-made or made by ET beings, they are bloody amazing! It's an incredible experience just to stand there and see the sheer size and symmetry of them, including the patterns and meanings of the shapes created.

Anyway, a few years ago, my sister and I were heading towards a particular crop circle and I had my dog with me. As we stepped into the circle, the dog would not settle and started acting very strangely indeed. I tried to stay there for a while and managed to take a picture of my sister roaming around, but eventually I decided I better go back to the car because my dog was not settling.

As soon as I got out of the crop circle, my dog was fine and happy to wander around. But he just would not go back in the crop circle. Later that day, we stopped for lunch and looked through the photos from that day. In the picture I had taken, there was a bright, white ball of light moving at a fast speed. It looked like someone had chucked a ball, and I had captured this speed because the light was stretched behind it.

Now, we hadn't seen this externally, but it was clearly there on the picture. And we knew that there were strange feelings inside the crop circle, because my dog knew. Perhaps he even saw it. I don't feel it was negative energy, but more the unknown energy of a completely different type of being.

I was amazed by this, and I still have this image now.

Years later, after following the reporting of crop circles, I decided to watch lots of videos about crop circle formation. I came across one where someone had filmed a crop circle being formed, and sure enough there were two white balls of light – exactly like the one in my picture – moving around whilst the shapes in the crops were forming. Who knows if this was real or not? People have different theories, but as I am a big believer of energy, I would like to say it is real. We are not alone, and as I always say, ENERGY IS EVERYWHERE AND ENERGY IS EVERYTHING.

I can't deny the energy I felt in that circle, and the orb would have brought that energy and those feelings inside me to trigger my clairs. If I had been more developed back then, I would have detected my clairs igniting more. However, now I do have all the tools and awareness to connect and understand how my clairs are being triggered.

Seeing energy within the atmosphere

I have had so much fun practising this one. For me personally, seeing energy in the atmosphere came in very strongly not long after my grandmother passed over. When I attended The International Academy of Consciousness for intensive OBE (Out of Body) training, I learned a lot more about the energy within the atmosphere and why I could externally see it.

It is very hard to explain, but imagine you are looking into thin air within a room with the heating on, and you see slight waves of heat yet they are transparent. That's what seeing energy can look like to most, if they are not aware of it, or if they are just starting to become aware of it. But when you start focusing on the energy in the atmosphere and going deeper with this, you will start to see this energy more strongly and for longer. We can even see this energy moving and merging.

This is not always spirit; it is sometimes energy. However, energy can still hold positive, neutral, or negative aspects and the type of energy will depend on how you feel when you see it. So again, it will be triggering those clairs inside of you (remember, we will discuss the other clairs in-depth later in the book).

We can also see energy movement within the dark. Imagine bubbles of energy but which merge and move so that they can mould into different shapes or waves of movement. They will always be moving, but this energy in the atmosphere is usually moving slowly. As I say, energy is everywhere and energy is everything, so ask yourself: what is thin air? Thin air is just a form of energy that we reside in. We have different densities of energy and different energy, from our physical living form to our auras to our spirit energy, and all of these different energies have become used to residing within the different densities and levels of energy in the atmosphere that surrounds us.

When we go out of our bodies, whether in dreams or actual controlled OBEs, we experience our spirit energy because we are no longer in our physical state. That is why it feels rather strange, because we are used to the psychical state of being. However, when in our spirit bodies, we can experience some profound connections with loved ones passed over. That's when it can really feel like we are with them, BECAUSE WE ARE. Spirit energy resides within the atmosphere that physical energy resides in; we just use a different density.

Moving back to the conversation of external clear seeing and seeing energy movement outside of our mind, this is energy's way of letting us know that we do have the ability to see other forms of energy if we really want to.

Statistics say that 80% of us are currently using only 15% of our brain capacity; some are using 20%; and some know how to move and merge out of their bodies into other states of consciousness, using a higher amount of their brain capacity. However, if we did use higher amounts, things would change a lot and we would not need shape and form and structure. So, somewhere down the line, humans decided to control and conform their brain capacity and keep it to a level that we can control. Through the centuries, humans and society started to believe this to be true, and so question all this stuff as weird or strange. To me, it's simple. As I've said, energy is everything and we are energy beings, so it makes complete sense that we can move and merge into different conscious states. This leads to the opinion that when we die we are not really dead. WE ARE LIVING – just in a non-physical way. We don't need our bodies any more until it's time for our next physical experience, and that is why and how our loved ones can be sitting next to us and chatting to us, even if their physical is no longer.

Seeing energy in the atmosphere exercise

Make yourself comfortable.

Whilst keeping your eyes open, take some deep breaths.

Begin to focus into thin air. Try not to focus on an object, just thin air.

Then make your eyesight go fuzzy. You will notice that your sight will haze in and out of being fuzzy and focused, but the trick is to not focus. Let what you are seeing become unfocused.

Keep holding that fuzzy. You may get a slight eye ache or headache, but that is normal.

Then see how everything in the room starts to morph into each other, and how things almost disappear or the different colours of objects within the room start to merge into just one colour.

You will notice the slight movements of the energy in the atmosphere, and from this you will also trigger your clairsentient, as you will start to feel certain things from the energy in the atmosphere.

TOP TIP

It is important to be aware that the things you feel or sense may not be negative; it could just be the unknown feeling of dropping into a different density of energy, which can sometimes scare us. But there is actually nothing to be scared of. It is simply the fear of the unknown.

Remember to write down what you saw and experienced so that you can look back at a later date. You can try this technique in different rooms or environments, and in daylight and night-time, and see how it changes.

Seeing auras

Everyone has a different aura, and our auras change over time depending on what we are going through in our lives. Likewise, with animals, plants, and land. For instance, if a plant is not being given enough water and is wilting, its aura might not be as bright and vibrant as when it is fully fledged and growing nicely. It works exactly the same with animals and humans.

Aura readings will show a picture of our auras almost as a large bubble around us, and we have different layers to our auras. Our outer layer often represents our current situation and the feelings we are experiencing at the moment.

The middle layer of our aura represents things that have been impacting or working through us for a much longer time.

And the deepest layer represents who we truly are, or things that are really deeply stuck within us. So, it's down to the aura reader to determine – using their other senses – what exactly the different colours mean for someone.

The way the aura bubble is pictured can change, and it may not be completely symmetrical over one's body. One side could be a different colour to the other side which, depending on what side, can also represent different things. There can also be patchy or hazy areas to one's aura, which again could represent some trauma. Our auras can also show emotional and physical trauma.

For instance, I have a bad shoulder from a sporting injury, and although I have had lots of chiropractic work over the years to reduce the pain, many of my students pick up on this in different hazy colours when we are practising reading auras with each other. So, if you are really listening to the senses you are getting in, you will receive information of why a part of someone's aura is a different colour, and you can push yourself to receive significant information on that one area.

You can see people's auras with your eyes open, but people don't always trust what they see so they find themselves closing their eyes. It is a natural habit, but if you can practise seeing auras with your eyes open it can be very interesting.

Knowing a simple colour chart can help, too. However, when working with colours we must trust our feeling about what the colours represent to us. If it's a lovely, pleasant colour, that will give us a soft, easy feeling, yet if it is a heavy, bold, or dark, erratic colour, that could make us feel something completely different.

Seeing auras exercise

Sit quietly with a family member or friend.

Make sure you haven't had a chat about what has been going on for them recently, so preferably pick someone you haven't seen for a while.

With eyes open, just start to look at them. And, as with the atmosphere energy technique, start to slightly haze out your eyesight and watch the different colours start to appear. You might only see them for a short while, or you might be able to hold those colours.

Become aware of where these colours are situated on the person's body.

Notice if some areas feel hazy or bright.

Notice what shades of the colour they are.

Do a whole body scan, and see if the colours change in different areas of their body.

Be really aware now of what you are feeling from each colour.

Begin to ask the question: why is this area that colour?

What does this colour mean?

Is this colour representing something emotional or physical?

Then start to tell them what you saw or felt. Remember, this will be triggering your other clairs to ignite, so you will now be feeling, hearing, sensing, or even seeing internally inside your mind, whilst also external seeing.

Then let the person confirm with you whatever you have described.

Write down your experiences and be really aware of how these thoughts and feelings were coming in for you.

TOP TIP ONE

Be really aware of the thoughts coming in, and don't block yourself if you question whether there really is a colour, or you are just thinking it. It is common for people to think that they are just making it up.

Have the guts to just speak out, and you will find that you have correctly picked up something about them.

TOP TIP TWO

This is best practised on people who we do not know a lot about. If we known them really well and everything happening in their lives, we can block ourselves by thinking that we already know the information we are seeing.

Chakras

Some aura reading pictures will also include the chakra colours down the body. Chakra charts have set colours for each chakra and exact meanings, and you can pick up on chakras during aura readings. However, chakras are energy points, and they can be impacted by things in one's life. Try not to get fixated on the colours of the chakras when doing the seeing aura exercise, because the colours can mean something completely different to the chakra meanings. You must go with your intuition, but by all means if you see the chakras or are drawn to them, do include them in your practice.

Chapter 4

Clairaudience – Clear Hearing

I'm sitting listening to the rain whilst writing this chapter, hearing the pitter patter of the raindrops gently hitting the window, and it's got me thinking about all the amazing sounds there are in the world, particularly those that make us feel good or help us to relax. There are also the sounds that bring emotions out in us, and sounds that make us remember periods of time or certain people, perhaps our loved ones passed over that we miss.

The rain brings back so many memories for me – ones which used to be hard, upsetting memories, but there are happy memories, too. It's funny how just a sound can TRIGGER something so deep within us.

Clairaudience

Definition: The power to hear sounds/voices and music said to exist beyond the reach of our ordinary earthbound experiences.

Clairaudience is an interesting sense, and one which a lot of people do not always realise they are using. The reason for this is that there are so many external noises in every given moment that it becomes difficult to detect other noises that are not of this earth. Like clairvoyance, we have two ways in which we receive our clairaudience. Clairaudience will predominantly be mediumship-based, but we can receive some sounds through our psychism, too. I have listed the ways we can receive below.

Firstly, Internal Clear Hearing:

- Voices in our mind.
- Sounds or noises in our mind.
- Music or singing in our mind.
- Tinnitus – JOINT CLAIRAUDIENCE.

Secondly, External Clear Hearing:

- Voices outside of our own body – when no physical form is around.
- Sounds or noises outside of our body – when no physical form is around, or sounds that would not make sense to us because of the surroundings we find ourselves in the time of the external noise.
- Music or singing outside of our body – again that cannot be explained by our current surrounds.
- Tinnitus – JOINT CLAIRAUDIENCE.

Joint clairaudience – this means that we can sometimes receive both internal and external clairaudience, usually starting with internal inside our mind – this will be called THE HUMM or BUZZING. This is very similar to tinnitus, and the hum or buzzing can be heard inside both ears, or one more strongly than the other. It starts as a ringing, buzzing, or humming, and we can sometimes get a physical sensation with this that starts it off. It can sound like we are underwater then transfer into the ringing/humming/buzzing. This can then turn into more of an external sound because of the way the noise vibrates through our mind/ear and outwards.

We always include tinnitus under clairaudience. Although there is a scientific, factual reason for tinnitus, there have been many theories that this is also connection from a spirit guide through our clairaudience, and why sometimes people suddenly start getting tinnitus.

I have a question for you. Have you ever noticed that you started getting tinnitus at a certain stage in your life, and you weren't sure why you kept getting it?

Well, perhaps ask yourself what was going on in your life when you started to get it.

Were you stressed?

Did you experience a loss of a loved one just before the tinnitus started?

If you can't remember when it started, but you know you have it, perhaps ask yourself these questions next time you are aware of it.

Which ear is it starting from? Left or right?

At the start of the book I talked about the meanings of the left and right side of our physical and energetic bodies, so this will help you to understand whether this is coming from a female or male source.

What were you just thinking of when it began?

Perhaps there is something you need to sort out in your life, or something you are questioning how to sort out.

When you can begin to trace and listen to this ringing in your ear, you can start to connect and understand which loved one/spirit guide is actually connecting with you at this time, and why. The why is usually based on what you were thinking about just beforehand, and they will be connecting to you to help with what you are questioning or thinking about.

Let me tell you about my tinnitus...

I was already well into and understanding my clairs and senses when my tinnitus set in. I was already working as a medium and a teacher, so my experience of tinnitus has been more recent. It started when I was thirty-one, about two months after my grandmother had passed over. Of course, I was already aware of other clairaudience I was receiving, but I hadn't experienced tinnitus before.

I was driving one day when I became aware of it in my left ear. So, because I am focused on my body and energy and how quickly the energy changes within me and my surroundings, I asked in my mind why I suddenly had this ringing in my left ear. I then listened to the first thoughts that came into my mind and felt my grandmother there. I knew it was definitely a female, because my left represents the females in spirit and my feminine side of my energy. Left also represents the past of us, so that's how I knew it was my grandmother – a female from my past.

I began to wonder why she had suddenly come through, and retraced my thoughts to what I had been thinking about when the tinnitus set in. I had been doubting something I wanted to create and do within my business. Realising this, I started to smile, because in that moment I had the overwhelming feeling that she was reassuring me not to doubt what I wanted.

Do you see how many thoughts I had in just a few moments, yet I was not aware of every negative thought that was running through my thought process at the time? I found it very interesting that I was able to get the message just from the tinnitus that occurred because it triggered other clairs within me. So now every time my tinnitus sets in, which it does usually every month – sometimes more often than other times, and always just in the left ear – I know there is a message. I then stop and listen/see/feel what the message is by tracing back to my original thoughts, and sure enough, it's usually when I am having doubts about something.

If you were not aware of this, you would just go to the doctor's and they would have an answer that might seem more believable. However, next time it happens to you, I suggest you ask yourself these questions and just see what you get.

A lot of people talk of having tinnitus after a loved one has passed over, but this isn't always the case. It could be that you are going through an awakening and waking up more to the spirit world.

Internal Clear Hearing – Voices in your mind

Ahhhhh, that famous 'hearing voices in my head' that has so often had you wondering if you were bloody crazy. Perhaps it has even freaked you out, especially if you don't recognise the voices. Maybe it's been when you're just drifting off into a cosy sleep and it shocks you into being wide awake. No matter what type of voice, it can be very alarming or very interesting. Whether it's a gentle whisper or a raging scream, we are always left wondering who it was. In many cases, we find ourselves shrugging the incident off and thinking we are just imagining it, but we can't deny what we heard or how it made us feel.

Whether we feel safe or not depends on what was said and the way it was said. Perhaps you recognise the voice, and you just know it's a loved one that you think of often. No matter what level your spirituality is at and whether you are aware of your clairaudience, you know deep down that these voices mean something.

We all hold the eight clairsenses within our energy bodies that travel through our physical body, but we maybe just haven't realised how much we are using them yet. That is why I decided to write this book. Through my teaching, I discovered that so many people ARE psychic, but they do not realise what senses are working for them. So, to understand and practise each clair in depth, we need to focus on each clair individually and really start detecting exactly how it is coming to us and then triggering each other clair.

Internal clear hearing is a great one, because learning specific techniques can really help us to shut out the world that is so loud and busy. That allows us to become calmer within the sound of stillness, and through this stillness we can enter into the sounds of the spirit realm.

Voices in our heads are just another way in which we receive. Of course, we have to be careful, because we need to be aware of our mental state of mind. But if we have lots going on and we can start to understand these voices and the energy around them, we can understand that we are probably NOT crazy.

I started to hear voices internally from a very young age, though I didn't realise this back then. My external clear seeing seemed to be much stronger than my other clairs, but as I got older I learned many amazing clairaudient techniques that blew me away and demonstrated how, through just a voice or sound, I was able to do a full reading.

Nice voices

We will hear different types of voices, including ones – as I said earlier – that we recognise and may bring us comfort and joy. Others we will not recognise, but we are still ok with the voices due to the energy of the voice and what it is saying. We will know this is not a loved one of ours, but it might be a loved one of someone we know or of the person we are reading for. We can also hear different languages, tones, and accents, in voices. We may hear them laughing, which makes us chuckle, but that in itself can have significance for the person who this spirit wants us to connect to. We might not be seeing the face to the voice, but we will get a sense of whether they are male or female, and old or young, due to the tone of the voice or the other senses now being triggered.

Nasty Voices

This will be every important, because we can sometimes feel scared or threatened and we will know quite quickly if this is not a nice spirit due to the tone and the way in which they speak to us. It is important, though, to understand the difference between a spirit being perhaps huffy or abrupt, to a spirit being nasty. If they are being nasty, it indicates that this spirit has bad intention – perhaps towards you, or to someone that you may know. If they are just abrupt or huffy, you will get the sense that this was possibly the way they were when alive, and doesn't necessarily mean they are here to be harmful.

If the voices are telling you to do something that doesn't feel right to you, this will be another indication that they have bad intention. If you are worried about this, you will need to learn various protection techniques or seek professional clearance from a medium who is fully aware and trained in this area.

I have experienced both positive and negative voices over my lifetime. Some were very nasty, and the experience felt quite dark. It's important to be responsible for your spirituality and your energy if you are actively training or learning within your spiritual journey, especially if you have strong mediumship. Again though, if you are not aware of these senses, you may find yourself in situations where people think you're crazy or you even think that yourself. However, through years of training, teaching, and clearing, I have become very, very aware that 85% of the time these voices can be cleared, and those people who heard them were not crazy.

Things like drinking heavily, taking drugs, heavy traumatic experiences that still impact us, accidents or operations, living in haunted houses, are all key things that lower our energies, leaving us more susceptible to negative spirit hanging around. So again, it's really important to be responsible for our physical and energetic self.

As I mentioned earlier, I had a drug addiction for four years back in my twenties. I inflicted this upon myself because of the sexual abuse I experienced through much of my childhood. Naturally, when I started taking drugs, I did not think I would become addicted and I didn't think I was doing it to cover the pain of my past trauma. It was through my journey of getting clean that I realised I had been intoxicating myself because I hated myself for what had happened to me.

Fortunately, I now know to love myself, and that has been a huge part of my transformation. I started to realise that the voices and sounds I heard when intoxicated were coming through so much stronger because my senses were heightened, although this is the wrong way to connect. Yet, when I became sober, the voices were still there. That's when I realised that actually it was never the intoxication; it was because my clairaudient was very strong.

For years I have now practised the safe way to connect in all manners. The problem with intoxicating yourself very heavily is that gaps are being created within your energy fields, so this is when more negative or draining energies can become stronger for you. And if you aren't aware of this, you can live a life worrying that you will always feel shit. Or you can become scared and fearful.

I'm not suggesting that you can't have a glass or two

of prosecco or a couple of beers, if you like, but I would advise that you do take responsibility for your energy. And if something you are hearing is becoming concerning for you, you will need to take action so that you feel better.

Externally hearing voices – this will feel similar to the voices in your mind, but they may be less common for you, and you will be able to tell the difference between hearing them externally to hearing them internally. We must not forget that sometimes we internally hear words in our own voice, and that's when things get really confusing. It just adds to us feeling crazy or can make us think we are just making things up. So again, it's really important to access the words that we are hearing within our own voice, because this will determine what the messages are and who they are from.

Hearing sounds and music

Similar to the voices, we may not notice the sounds and noises as much; hearing music or singing will usually be more noticeable. But again, it's important to understand why and where the sounds or music are coming from. The most common time to hear music or singing is usually when you are drifting off to sleep or when you are coming out of a sleep and still in a dozy state.

I remember one morning I was in and out of a sleepy state when I heard a beautiful humming/singing sound. It seemed to be far in the distance, rather than in my mind, so I knew I was hearing externally, but I knew it was spirit because of the way it was sounding. You see, the sounds might be really clear, but it's the energy of the sound which again triggers the feelings. When you are in a dozy state, you are residing in a different density of energy at that time, which makes it easier for spirit to connect. So, you will feel the difference in energy, and that's how I knew the beautiful humming was spirit.

Sounds are so interesting when they kick in through our clairaudience, as we can sometimes be surprised because we might not expect a particular sound. However, sometimes our loved ones will make the same sound each time they visit, and that can act as a sign that they are with us at that very moment.

Internal clear hearing sound exercise Mediumship

You will need to sit with someone else who you are practising on (make sure they know information about their loved ones passed over, so they can confirm with you after).

Close your eyes.

Take some deep breaths.

Quiet your mind.

Focus on the sounds that you hear within the room. Really become aware of each and every sound, and just be with them for a moment.

Now bring your attention to the sounds that are outside the building you are in, like cars on the road, people passing by, kids playing, birds tweeting, the weather, any roadworks. Just be really aware and in the moment with those sounds outside.

See if they become stronger or if they start to fade out.

Now take your attention to further away. Imagine the sounds from up the street or around the block, and see if you actually hear any sounds from there. Be really aware of whether you can hear them and what they are.

Now imagine white light starting to cascade around you, and see yourself stepping into this white light which takes you further and beyond, away from the everyday sounds you experience.

Then ask in your mind for a loved one of the person you are sitting with to give you a sound that relates to them in some way.

Listen to the sound within your internal hearing, no matter how random or strange the sound may be.

Now begin to access this sound and see how it triggers your other clairsenses.

When you hear the sound, has it now brought a visual into your mind?

Has it made you think or feel anything in particular?

Are you able to detect whether this sound is linked to this loved one's job or hobby? And if so, how are you receiving this? Vision? Thought? Sense? Feeling? Emotion? Smell? More hearing?

Now see what else you pick up on based on that first sound. Perhaps you get a good sense of the love one's personality, or maybe even pick up on how they passed. Perhaps the sound is part of a memory that they want to show you so that the person you are practising on can resonate with who you are connecting to.

Then, when you are ready, take a deep breath and bring yourself fully and safely back into the room.

Tell the other person what you first heard and how it all then was received, and get them to give you clarification of any of the information.

TOP TIP ONE

Remember that the sound may only be very brief, and if so, you can either ask for the sound again or access what happens next via your other clairs igniting and allowed to flow.

TOP TIP TWO

Remember, if you are unsure, just ask the question in your mind and say in your mind, 'I'm unsure, can you please give me that sound again?'

TOP TIP THREE

Remember that there could well be no clarification from the person you are practising on. This can make you feel that you didn't do something right or that you failed. We must remember that whatever we receive always represents something, but the sitter might not be aware of what the significance is. We need to remind them to check with other family members or friends, and to have an open mind.

I have been a medium long enough and trusted my senses and the messages coming through enough to know that each and every time it will mean something somehow to the sitter in front of me. So please bear this in mind when you are at beginner's stage and double check the questions in your mind, or ask the sitter to check with others who may know. Nine times out of ten they will end up getting back to you because another family member has clarified something you said to them, or the information suddenly clicks in their own mind and they let you know. I have had people come back to me years later to confirm things, and even though it took a long time, I still received clarity in the end. Nevertheless, I TRUSTED what came in at the start. TRUSTING is one of the biggest barriers when developing spiritually, especially when doing mediumship, and that's due to individual confidence levels.

That is why it is so important to practise the techniques and really hone each clair, because it will strengthen your psychism, and mediumship, and intuition, and you will feel so much clearer and more confident.

The first time I ever tried a technique like the one above, I had a brilliant experience. Let me tell you about it...

I was working with a nice man as my practice partner, but I didn't know him at all. As I started to focus on the sounds, I found it very peaceful and was able to zone out of the everyday noises; it felt like a disconnection from this physical world into the outer worlds. I was already quite used to stepping into a spiritual realm or the space of white light, so I felt the disconnection and connection very strongly.

As I welcomed the noise/sound of a loved one linked to the man sitting front of me, I heard a whistle, but it was as if someone was whistling a tune. Straight away, I listened to my claircognizance (clear knowing) and knew this was a man. I then started to get internal clairvoyance, and I saw a foggy day which I sensed was early morning. I saw a field, then more sounds started to come in. I was keen to keep focusing on the clairaudient technique at hand, but allowed the other senses to ignite to tell me more.

The next sound I heard was a crispy, crunching sound, as if someone was walking on icy ground, which went hand-in-hand with the foggy morning visual. I then heard keys rustling, and from the sound I got, I sensed it was a large bunch of keys. I felt these were work keys and that this man worked outside in the field I was seeing. I then heard the keys unlocking and the sound of a metal fence being opened.

At that point, I received another visual – this time, of a wide, metal fence opening. I could also hear laughing and a cockney accent starting to come in, so I could then tell that this man was quite funny and liked to have a laugh and exchange banter. I felt as though he wanted to banter with the man I was practising on.

I started laughing, because he was making me laugh. I saw a visual of this man now; I could see he was around forty years old, and he was smiling. He then showed me a tree in this field during this foggy, frozen morning. By that point, the sounds had stopped, and I was receiving more internal clairvoyance which ignited other senses.

Suddenly, I got a strong sensation around my throat, which felt like I couldn't swallow or breathe, then I saw a quick flash of him hanging. I knew that this man had taken his own life.

Afterwards, when I'd finished, I discovered that this loved one had been my sitter's good friend, and he had hanged himself where he worked as a groundsman. That explained the big set of keys which he used to open the gate everyday, and how I had sensed that this took place early in the morning.

My sitter confirmed that the man had always been very funny and that it was his cockney accent I had heard. Apparently, he had always loved that particular tree, so it made sense that he took his life there; it was also a quiet area so it was unlikely anyone would interrupt him taking his life.

However, when the man was communicating to me, he was showing me he was happy and had wanted to go, but he wanted to tell his friend that he was ok, that he loved him, and thanked him for being a good mate.

I remember being stunned that I had got all of that from one initial sound. But if you practise and you access every single thing coming in, you will find that you actually receive a lot of information. And if you access and become aware of it all, you will create the space to understand your senses and the messages and connection even more, and you will be able to strengthen this.

Externally Hearing Sounds/noises/music

As I briefly explained earlier, hearing sounds outside of your physical head is very different, although you will still feel that mysterious or etheric feel to the sounds, whether they are nice or unpleasant. Obvious places of hearing externally could be when you are in haunted buildings or places that have a lot of history, like castles, old towns, monuments, old pubs, graveyards, churches, etc. You might hear sounds like voices, singing, laughing, music, footsteps, or echoes, perhaps even children playing. Places like woodlands can often hold the sounds of spirit, too.

Whatever you hear, you must know that the sound will be followed by a sense, feeling, visual, etc, so it's important to access those next senses kicking in to know whether you feel safe or unsafe. REMEMBER, though, we can make ourselves feel unsafe due to the unknown feeling we are sensing, but that does not necessarily mean that what we are hearing is harmful. So, practise accessing the energy behind the sounds to really help you to understand whether this might just be the sound of a lost soul who actually needs help.

Always know you are and can be protected; it is completely your choice and within your control. If we put out the frequency that we are not safe or we are scared, then some energy and some spirit can sense that and be drawn to that.

The external sounds will often be the sounds of spirit that is stuck; a lost soul that didn't make it to the light. If they made it to the light, they will often bring you internal clear hearing noises and sounds. The reason lost souls will bring external hearing is because they are still stuck in the physical realm, so they have not been able to be released fully from their physical form. Some know they are stuck, and some do not; some will be innocent and lovely. Others can be innocent but aggravated, and this will be because they haven't gone through the release process of moving to the light. So if someone was often aggressive in their physical life, they may still come across like that to us, but it doesn't mean they are an evil spirit. It's important to know the difference.

Some will be more of a darker nature and will want to remain stuck so that they can continue to pester or even torment people in the physical. They sometimes feed off people who are alive, and know exactly what they are doing.

Be prepared that some external sounds can be quite terrifying. If you do hear or sense anything that does alarm you, it's best to seek a professional medium to help to clear it. Whether innocent or not, each and every spirit deserves to go back home to the light. If it's a lost soul that you hear and they are cleared, you will not hear them again in the internal. But if it's a loved one, you will hear from them in some way again.

I have heard many external noises and sounds, some of which have been interesting, and others which alarmed me years before I was a medium. I used to hear footsteps running up and down the same hallway in a house I lived in, and always at the same time of night. So, you will find that there is sometimes a pattern to the external sounds you hear, and again this can all depend on the soul that's stuck. Perhaps they only remember a particular part of their life. For instance, when my mum went to clear the footsteps noise, I already knew this was a young girl from the Victorian era and it felt like her footsteps were hurried. I would feel distressed – not at the thought that she was going to harm me, but because I felt the spirit's distress at what she felt in her physical life. When Mum did the clearing, she found that this young girl was running away from a man who would taunt and scare her. Thankfully, my mum was able to help heal this moment and release the girl from this pain so that she could move through to the light.

You can sometimes hear people crying, and this might be because they are crying for the loss of someone and they don't know how to find them, even though they are dead themselves. Trauma and situations that deeply hurt people can also result in souls becoming stuck, so they just need help to understand this.

There was a lady in one of the house clearings which my mum and I attended (this was when I had now learnt how to do clearings), and she kept crying. The woman who lived there would get so upset and scared because she would hear whimpering, screaming, and crying, coming from the smaller bedroom. When I connected to her, I could see the lady wrapped in a blanket, very upset, looking for her baby. However, her baby had died, so we guided her to understand that her baby was in the light and that she could go there, too. It took some time, because she was sure her baby was still in the room and she was very confused. She had never got over the loss of her baby, and that had kept her stuck earthbound when she eventually died.

She did go to the light, after some healing, and was able to reconnect with her baby, which was beautiful and – for us – really fulfilling. The lady who owned the house has never heard the crying since, and was very relieved but also quite touched by what we had picked up. She told us later that what we described made a lot of sense, because since she had moved there she kept having dreams of her own son – who's living –dying. Now she began to understand that she had been picking up on this other lady, who had been stuck there for so long.

Never underestimate the sounds you hear. Always ask yourself what a sound means. A sound, whether external or internal, can lead to a beautiful connection and a story that needs to be told.

Chapter 5

Clairsentience – Clear Sensing

Clairsentience: From the late 17th century French, *clair* ('clear') and *sentience* ('sensing') The psychic ability of a person to acquire knowledge by means of sense.

Aww, the good old clear sense. Although it seems pretty obvious from the word 'sense', this is a tricky one because so many people get it mixed up with the clairempathy sense (clear feeling/emotion). So when I hear students or clients describing their sentient with the words 'I just get a feeling', that's where they 'go wrong in accessing which clair is igniting for them. You see, sense and feeling are different, yet very similar.

Question: What is a feeling to you? Be really, really clear when you ask yourself this question. To me, a feeling is either physical or an emotion that we actually FEEL within our bodies when connecting to one's energy, whether alive or in spirit.

A sense is not a feeling; you DON'T feel a sense. You know that you sense something about someone, but can you remember actually feeling a sense?

So, there is a definite difference. Someone who is more clairsentient will sense someone has pain around their knee from injuring it years ago. Yet someone who is more clairempath will physically feel the pain within their own knee, and will access that the pain is from a previous injury.

Someone who is clairsentient will sense that someone is still heartbroken from a break-up, whereas a clairempath will emotionally feel that heartache in their own heart. This is why people get so mixed up with these two clairs.

Of course, we can hold both clairsentient and clairempath within us, and either or both senses can be trained to become stronger.

When we can really understand the difference, how these clairs are working within us, and how to distinguish which one is kicking in, when, and why, it will help to get us to a more intuitive and stronger position within our energy system, therefore helping us to be stronger psychics and mediums.

We can then offer so much more to people, whether we are professional readers, healers, teachers, or just giving some kind words of wisdom to help in some way. We can genuinely change people's lives in very positive ways by the messages that we give them.

I became really interested in the clairs when I was having such strong connection with different spirits. I was keen to understand how and why I was experiencing so many different sensations. As I have explained before, learning and honing each clair for myself has been fundamental to the way I am as a spiritual being and as a teacher. And I have seen first-hand the benefits of how really understanding them in-depth has helped me achieve so much.

My next question: Do you want to have senses and do a good job sometimes? Or do you want to be fully in control of your senses, and do a BRILLIANT job every single time?

I think I know the answer to that one. And if it's the second option, then I would definitely allow yourself to start accessing the difference between every clair, but especially between clairsentient and clairempath.

Clairsentience can often seem like we are using all of our senses, because of the way it triggers every other clair that we have. Our senses make use of the energies, vibrations, and emotions of those around us. The traits of a clairsentient is, by their very nature, to usually be a gentle soul and a good listener. They are not attention-seekers; they are observers who prefer to witness rather than being witnessed. They are deep souls, and usually quiet. They can become drained easily, too. They can sense a change in energy within environments, or people, or even animals and plants. Does this sound like you?

Quite often, clairsentience is the overlooked sense, because clairvoyance is usually so strong and common in shape or form within most people. And, of course, people believe something more if they have strong visuals and those visuals come true or make sense. People like to have grand visuals, so if someone is more clairsentient rather than any of the other clairs, it can sometimes seem like guess work – unless they study their clairsentience streak and start to recognise how it unfolds for them.

There are no techniques to perfect your clairsentience specifically, however, many techniques within the other clairs will most likely highlight your clairsentience. So, it will be down to you to see whether you notice it within you when doing spiritual development.

TOP TIP

When practising the other techniques in this book, write by the side of each technique whether you noticed the clairsentience kicking in, and HOW it came through.

It will usually come in on the back end of some of the other clairs igniting your sense, but make sure it is clairsentient and not clairempathy that is kicking in.

Chapter 6

Clairempathy – Clear Empathy

Clairempathy: From the late 17th century French, *clair* ('clear') and *empathy* ('feeling and emotion')
The psychic ability of a person to acquire knowledge without knowing how they acquired it.

Awwww, the wonderful EMPATH – now, this is one of my favourite clairs, most probably because I have had so any amazing – and also uncomfortable – experiences within empathy. There are so many levels to empathy, so understanding how to break it down is a good place to start.

Following on from the brief description in the clairsentience chapter about empathy, there are two forms of empathy and lots of obvious ways to distinguish between the two. However, most people will not realise that it's not actually their own energy. So, they will feel a pain or emotion and then think they are ill, but we MUST question why we suddenly started to feel ill. What were we doing? Where were we? Who have we just spoken to? When we can understand the difference in energies and how this transfers to us, we can be better equipped to pick up on the pain or emotions of others but also to make sure we are not left with it. This will be less draining and will also make us feel safe.

The two types of clairempathy are as follows:

Clairempathy – Physical: Feeling physical symptoms, conditions, pains, aches, uncomfortable sensations, and physical reactions to bodily sensations, both inside the body and on the outer layer of the body.

Clairempathy – Emotional: Feeling a wide range of emotions from negative to positive.

If you are an empath, you might experience one of these more than the other, or you may experience both. A physical pain could begin within your body, which could then trigger an emotion linked to that pain. For instance, if someone had M.S. you might feel the symptoms within your body, which could then make you feel the emotion of being fed-up or deflated.

We can pick up on physical and emotional energies of those still alive and those passed over, as well as animals and plants/land. W can also pick up on the empathy in places, however it will be the energy of what happened in that place, or spirit that is stuck and still resides there.

Having empathy is another very common clair for many people. We all have the ability to have this sense and strengthen it, but some of us may not want to if our clairempathy is very strong, because it can feel uncontrollable, scary, and even confusing – particularly if it happens suddenly, when we were feeling great beforehand.

However, if we can understand this sense in great depth, it can be a great way to really help people. You see, if you can really get how someone feels deep inside and let them know that, you can help them to feel that they are truly heard.

The levels of empathy are very in-depth, with many layers y and aspects to think about and question so that we can fully understand what is going on.

Clairempathy – Physical

- Pains
- Symptoms and conditions
- Sensations and Reactions

Pains

Ahhhhhh, the dreaded pain chat. Have you ever been having a nice coffee with a friend, and you come away and realise you have a pounding headache? You find yourself questioning why you have a headache when you were fine before. So, you put it down to being busy or maybe just feeling a bit off. But perhaps this headache is excruciatingly painful with sharp jabbing pains, so you become worried and start thinking the worst. You might even get annoyed with yourself because it's getting in the way of the rest of your day, stopping you from doing the things you need to do because you really need to lie down. You take some painkillers to try and get rid of it, but they don't reduce the pain at all.

Little did you know that you could have got rid of that headache the second it entered your energy… because this head pain was actually linked to the friend you had coffee with earlier. Perhaps if you had been aware of this energy entering at the time it did, you could have realised that you were picking up on someone else's pain and had the chance to ask them. That would have given you clarity that, sure enough, they had been experiencing migraines.

But what if that friend, when you asked them, said they were fine and had no headaches at all? That would leave you feeling rather lost about the head pain. Consider then that perhaps this was actually the physical pain of a loved one passed over who is linked to this friend? Maybe a parent, or grandparent, or another relative or friend. And the person you were with probably wouldn't connect that you were actually picking up on their loved one.

This is where the physical empathy can then trigger other senses to come in, and if you are aware of the other senses and what you are thinking, seeing, hearing, etc, then you may be able to actually pass a message on.

Another option in this scenario could be that the friend says they don't have a headache, and when you ask if it could be a loved one linked to them, they again say no. You can see how this gets really confusing, because you have two options both with a big fat no, leaving you even more confused. The next thing to consider is perhaps this is an ancestor of theirs that they really know nothing about. If you think to suggest this, maybe you could guide them to ask other people who may know, and that would possibly connect some of the dots together for you.

If this option still does not work, I would look at the

environment that you were in when you came away with that awful headache. You see, energy can be transferred from one person to another in just a mere passing moment. Just like energy can be transferred from a person to an object or a piece of furniture, it can reside within or around the item for some time. So, if you are going to a busy coffee shop, be aware that, throughout the days, weeks, months, years, it has seen thousands of people with their different physical issues and emotions sit in that same chair. You just may have well picked up this energy and it briefly attached to you.

This is really important to understand, because if you go deeper into this thought process you can now see that means there is energy everywhere, whether positive or negative, physical or emotional. It's on every button you press, everything you touch and hold. For instance, money from the cashpoint or from the till in a shop – just think how many hands it has passed through.

This is where it can get scary for some, like it did for me. I was such a strong empath that I started to fear touching things and even worried about passing people in the street. I didn't want to shake anyone's hand or hug anyone! That is when I KNEW I was an empath, but I didn't then know sufficient protection or techniques to clear energies.

Before I became aware that I was an empath, I would experience extreme physical pains – to the point where it scared me. Sometimes I thought I was dying, but tests and examinations would all show there was nothing wrong. The pains I felt were so strong, yet the healthcare professionals weren't taking me seriously. Some even hinted that I had some mental health issues instead, and that perhaps I was obsessed with thinking there was something wrong with me. One even suggested I was a hypochondriac. However, my intuition, my CLAIRSENTIENT was telling me differently. Even though I didn't register my clairsentient kicking in at that time, I knew deep down that there was an answer to all of this. I wasn't crazy, and I truly was feeling this awful pain.

Some of the pains triggered emotional stuff in me, and there were times I felt all over the place. Think of any type of pain someone can experience, and it's possible you could pick up on it – anything from just a tiny cut to a massive brain tumour, or sudden heart attack that killed someone straight away, illnesses like cancer pains, a sore throat, giving birth, period cramps, or even broken bones.

The problem with pain is there are so many factual scientific reasons why and what the pain is for someone, so we often put less serious things like a headache, a sore throat, or just a bit of back pain, down to tiredness or stress, or that we are coming down with something. In these cases, it will be harder to determine what is actually our own energetic pain. Of course, if you are experiencing extreme heart pains yet the doctors are saying everything is fine, that will be more confusing for us.

The smaller pains can sometimes be harder to miss. Think about all the times we have taken some painkillers or even a course of medicine to resolve pain, and it hasn't worked. We might not have even needed to take anything, because the pain was never our own.

This is why it's so important that we truly and wholly know our own individual energy, so that we can feel new energies coming into our physical form, to be able to send them away immediately and not suffer that pain. Or so that we can use that pain to connect and pass on a message that needs to be given.

When I'm providing readings, sometimes I will feel pain all the way through, but I put myself in the position of mental mediumship and allow this pain in as a trigger point to ignite my other clairs and I can access the psychic or loved ones' messages. And once I acknowledge and get clarification on that pain, it goes away. If it persists, that's usually an indication that the loved one hasn't been acknowledged or that the message has not been understood. I then have to work to understand fully what I need to pass on, because I will not want this pain to be over me.

However, if it still persists, I will say to the spirit – or my angels, if it's pain from someone alive – to please remove this pain that does not belong to me.

You have the right to release it, because it does not serve your own energy long-term.

Let me tell you a powerful pain story of my own...

I was sitting doing a reading in my earlier days and became aware of a man in spirit coming forward. As he approached, I started to feel a lot of agonising pain; a stabbing sensation in stomach. Not only was I physically feeling this strong stabbing pain, but I also felt my whole body hurting as if I was being tortured. Suddenly there was intense pain over my neck and head. It was awful.

However, as I explained each pain and how it was

happening, the lady having the reading told me it made a lot of sense to her. I knew from the pain that this man had been murdered. Not only that, but he had been on the run for days and the men who murdered him had been following him, hunting him down. Naturally, these physical feelings triggered other clairs within me to ignite, like the internal clear seeing clairvoyance and also the clairempathy – emotional side, because I started to feel the anxiety and the stress, worry and fear, but also the anger about the whole situation.

I was able to provide a whole lot of detail to the lady, whose brother was the man speaking to me. If I hadn't accessed the full picture by listening to these pains and then allowing the other clairs to trigger, I could have missed some key points. The trick is to not be scared of the pain you feel. Don't hold the emotions back either, because this helps the sitter to really understand that you are connected to their loved one in that very moment.

The neck and head pain was where his head had been battered in-between a door. The stabbing pain was, of course, him being knifed over and over, and the heaviness was him being dragged through a derelict factory somewhere abroad. I knew he was being tortured because there was too many sudden pains all over my body. Yes, this was an awful way to die, but the man was actually at peace. He was a very funny character and upbeat to his sister, with lots of love in his heart coming through. This showed me that, despite his traumatic passing, he actually did pass to the light properly and didn't become stuck, which can happen in some cases of murder.

My partner's father sadly passed away a few years ago. He

suffered a brain tumour, and every time he pops in to give guidance, I feel the same head pain in the exact same space. This sharp, intense pain then makes me feel clouded and confused. The head pain affects me in the exact place where his tumour was, and he did become very confused at the end.

When I experience head pains, I can understand how some people struggle to think straight, because the pain is so uncomfortable. But when it does happen to me, I do know to ask: Is this my confusion? Then I usually get: 'NO, it isn't. It's theirs.'

My partner's father is so lovely. He was a mechanic, and I have found that he seems to come through mostly if there are car issues. My partner is also a mechanic, and he worked with his father for many years. I, on the other hand, do not have a fucking clue about cars and am not interested in the slightest about types of cars or anything to do with them. So, I definitely do not know how to fix them.

One evening, when that head pain came over me, I centred myself for a moment and said hello to his father, then asked what he wanted to say. He told me that he had been around my partner a lot that day, but when I told my partner this he didn't really seem to listen to me; he had his back to me, sitting on the bed taking his shoes off. I said to his dad, in my mind, 'He isn't listening to me. I don't think he believes you're here right now. Can you please tell me or show me something that will get him to trust that you are here right now?'

So, his father then showed me my partner's work van with the right-hand indicator constantly blinking and that it wouldn't stop. He also showed me my partner in his work clothes, getting in and out of the van, looking under the wheel, and doing a few tests of some sort to maybe detect what was wrong with the indicator.

When I told my partner that his dad was showing me all of this, he quickly turned round and gave me his full attention. 'Is my dad telling you that?' he asked. I said, 'Yes, he's showing me that he was with you in the van.' My partner then explained that earlier that day, his van's right indicator had done exactly what I had explained and that no-one else knew about it.

That is now one of the moments my partner will never forget, because the information I gave him was so significant to him, and he truly knew and trusted that his dad was with him. It really made his day. That all started with the physical head pain, and look how happy I made him. I also made his father happy, because he was able to continue doing what he loved which was helping out with the cars.

As mediums, we are here to help our loved ones not only pass on guidance but to also tell the story of their life. When we can give that to loved ones – whether we knew them or not – it is the most amazing feeling for us, and them. It also helps you to develop your skillset even more.

Bless my partner's father. Malcolm, your soul lives on amongst those that love you, and I will always respect you and be grateful for the time I did know you physically.

Symptoms and Conditions

Symptoms again are key pointers to our physical empathy sense. Symptoms are not under the pain category because the symptoms we feel are not always painful. Again, they can be confusing for us, because they can be ever so mild, or they can be very strong. The symptoms that we feel from others can persist or can last just a few seconds, so can be hard to catch. As with pains, the symptoms can also be missed because we might just put them down to a common issue – many have like a nauseous sensation. However, I ask my students: How long have you felt this? When did it start? Did it begin after being around someone? Or in a particular place you visited? Are you assessing your true energy?

Symptoms and conditions can include things like itchy skin, itchy scalp, strange sensations within the body or on the outside layer of our body, sore throats, tickly coughs, throbbing feelings, sore eyes, swollen feelings – anything you can possibly think of which might be annoying but not painful.

For instance, I once did a reading for a lady, and I had her grandmother come through. I began to scratch my head because it felt very itchy. It was not painful, but I was feeling the emotion of irritation kicking in with the physical feeling of itchiness. I decided to ask the grandmother in spirit about the itchy head, and she told me that her scalp was really flaky as she got older and she lost a lot of hair, so she decided to wear wigs. However, the wigs made the itching worse because her head would get hot, but she refused to have her head on show with the flakes showing. From that, I got that she always took a lot of pride in how she looked. Even when she was really poorly, she wanted her family members to make sure her wig was on.

When I mentioned this to the lady having the reading,

she started to cry because she could completely relate to what had been said. She made a loving joke about her grandmother always wanting her wig on, and we had a really good laugh about it. Her grandmother was laughing, too. It's so lovely that these things make special moments of connection with our loved ones. I have never forgotten that feeling of itchiness, and it started with that feeling.

Conditions, again, are very similar, but these could be more ongoing for someone, or leading to something that ends up being more of a health issue for the loved one. Conditions can also be mental, too, so this also crosses into emotional empathy.

Sensations and Reactions

Sensations will be the feelings we experience due to the health issues or pains from a person or spirit. For instance, if someone was feeling sick just before they passed, you might pick up this sicky feeling up and carry it. As I've mentioned, it's so important to assess when you started feeling sick or strange. Who were you with? Where did you visit? Because if it persists, it could well be a spirit trying to get through to you, and they are being persistent because they know that you aren't realising it. With sicky feelings, we often just put this down to us feeling unwell, but there are different levels of sickness and we must question what type of sick feeling it is and why it has come on so strongly all of a sudden.

Other times, sensations could be ones we can physically feel like being burning or freezing cold, nausea, numbness of the body, skin, nerve sensations, muscular feelings, gut pains, sniffling, and even cravings for or sudden dislikes to food – anything that is not painful but feels strange or uncomfortable.

We have reactions to the sensations that come over us. For instance, the nauseous feeling might mean we think we are actually going to be sick, so the reaction will be a physical reaction of gagging or trying to hold it in, which then pulls at our throat or stomach.

Let me tell you a very interesting story about a sensation and reaction experience I had once...

One Friday afternoon, I had been to the next town to me – about a 20-minute drive from my home – to drop off something I had made, which a lady was purchasing. This was in my very early days of readings, so I was still getting used to putting up sufficient protection around me. I had dropped off the item, collected the money, and was back in my car driving home.

I quickly noticed that I was suddenly feeling very sick. This feeling ignited my clear taste sense (clairgustance), and I could taste vomit very strongly; this clear taste sense then kickstarted my clear empathy emotional, and I began to feel scared and anxious and as if I needed to hurry. I felt I was being followed and I noticed that my reaction to the initial sick feeling was that I was now very anxious and driving to the point where I felt pretty desperate. It was strange, because it was a mixture of rushing because I felt

I was going to be sick, but also because I felt I was being chased in the car.

I then did my checks and asked if this was linked to the lady I had just visited. I saw a flash of a woman and I knew she was the lady's mother. So, I said to her, 'You are going to have to stay with me until I've finished driving, because there is nowhere to pull over. But you need to release the sickness and anxiety from me.' Once I said that, I was able to drive more calmly, but I then had a strong smell (clairalience) kick in of chip shop chips and gravy!

Now, I can't stand the gravy from chip shops, but I do like chip shop chips. And this craving was so strong that my reaction was to get to the first chip shop I could see and buy the chips and gravy. At the time I was experiencing a lot of hypos from my hypoglycaemia, which I do know was my own health issue, so I wasn't eating things like chips. However, the craving was so strong that I just had to indulge. I bought the chips and sat and gobbled them up in the car like I'd never eaten before.

Knowing that this lady was still with me and that this was her actual craving she was putting upon me, I finished up the chips then spoke to her to find out the full story of what happened to her and why she was so sick and rushing. She told me that she was in a car chase, trying to get away from the police; she was also a heroin addict and had been experiencing sickness a lot, leading to her passing. When they crashed, she had physically been sick over herself, so that's the way she had been found. That all made a lot of sense to me. I asked her about the chips, which she clearly loved, and she told me it was her favourite meal and something she would eat every Friday afternoon.

I knew she was grateful for what I had done, but I told her that she must stay with her daughter and not follow me. She told me that her daughter cried over her and didn't realise she was there. I offered to pass on a message to her daughter, and she asked me to tell her that she had seen her granddaughter, and she's beautiful, and would be coming to her daughter.

I messaged the lady when I got home. I really did not know this lady from Adam and had spent mere moments handing over the item she'd bought from me, so I had no information about her at all. I thought she might be offended if I just randomly messaged her about her mother, but I trusted that it would be ok.

When I told her everything I had experienced, she confirmed the car accident with vomit over her mother, along with the addiction and the chips every Friday. She also told me that no-one knew, but just before I dropped off the item, she had done a pregnancy test and it was positive. She had been crying because she wished her mum was there to see her kids. Of course, she couldn't confirm the sex at that time, but months later she did, and sure enough her baby was a girl, who has been born and is well and healthy. This message touched the lady so much and brought her a lot of comfort. She feels now that her mother is around her and her children, and it brings her much happiness.

After this situation, and the way I felt and reacted, I decided to seriously up my protection level, because although it had been an amazing outcome, I had genuinely felt scared and very sick, and I wouldn't have eaten something that didn't agree with me. Since then, I have had training and practice to put in sufficient protection.

The physical and emotional senses are great, because they can kickstart a whole story of a loved one or really help bring comfort to the person alive and the loved one passed over. However, it's really important to have your protection up, because if I hadn't already been aware of my senses or thought to check what was going on, I might have crashed or even been physically sick. I might even have remained scared, with a strong sensation lasting a lot longer, which would have interfered with my life. So, not only did this help these two women but it helped me to set I stone a new, stronger part of my spiritual development.

Sometimes it's ok to allow the sensation to help understand the message, and at least the woman got to experience her favourite meal one last time.

Clairempathy – Emotional

- Emotions of all variations
- Characteristics
- Sensations and reactions

Now we include the emotions under this chapter. As discussed earlier, the physical empathy can kickstart the emotional empathy and vice versa, so depending on whatever clair is igniting depends on how the emotions come to us. The emotions could come first with no physical feelings at all, and no visuals or other senses, so this is where it can get confusing. We can be feeling fine within ourselves during our day and then suddenly feel extremely down, angry, deflated, etc. As I've mentioned before, this is when it's so important to assess where you have just visited. Who have you just been with? Or spoken to? We can pick up emotions from people, spirit, places, animals, even land and plants, but if it's people then it doesn't matter where in the world they are. You might simply look at a picture of someone on social media and start to feel what that person is feeling. Likewise, you can look at a picture of someone passed over, and again you might feel the emotions they carried with their life when they were alive.

Why, you may ask, do spirit still hold emotions? Firstly, just to reassure you, if someone picks up emotions – or physical pains, for that matter – from someone passed over, it DOES NOT MEAN they still feel this way. They are usually at peace and happy. However, our spirit bodies reside within our physical form until death, so our spirit body collects the blueprint of emotions and feelings over time. For instance, if someone was very depressed when alive, it would make sense if a medium picked this up and the sitter would resonate with that. So, it will not always upset someone to hear about that, because perhaps their loved one was depressed or grumpy their whole life.

Likewise, if someone was always very kind and loving, then the medium may feel overwhelmed with the emotion of love, and again, the sitter will be able to resonate with this if that's how their loved one was.

It's the more negative emotions that disturb us humans. And if we're not realising that this is actually emotion from someone else or from spirit, we can start thinking that perhaps we are crazy, up and down emotions making us question if we have bipolar disorder. It can really interfere with our very being, and can be hard to detect if we have been that way for a long time, or if our feelings are considered normal. But even if there are scientific facts that might explain it, we know deep within ourselves that something doesn't feel right.

This is where we do have to be careful, because some of us do actually have mental health issues that, for whatever reason, we may have needed to experience in this life. However, if we are picking up on others' thoughts and emotions, we can perceive these as our own. I have so many stories of feeling others' emotions – alive and passed over – and when I have detected and realised what's happening, I have been able to understand what exactly is my own and what is definitely not mine.

There is a big difference between what is within us and what is around us. The problem is that this big difference is clouded over time from consumption of what is all around us emotional-wise.

Let me tell you about an emotional experience linked to spirit I once had that was not mine...

I went on holiday with my partner and children to the Costa del Sol. As a very in-tune medium by that point, in the corridor leading to our room I could pick up a young woman who was in spirit walking the corridor, so I knew she was stuck – as in, not passed over to the light properly.

I decided not to communicate with her because, although this skillset is switched on all the time and sometimes when out and about or on holiday, I just wanted to enjoy the time with my family. So, I simply did some more of my protection. Two days later, after settling into our holiday, I went to the local cocktail bar to listen to a band. The cocktails were very strong, and I found myself a little sozzled.

On the walk home, I was happy and singing with my family, and when we got into the hotel room I went to bed. In the middle of the night, I woke up quite disorientated and saw the woman in spirit standing by my bed. I remember saying in my head that she must leave the room and let us sleep. I woke up the next morning with a very sore throat and feeling like I had been hit by a bus, and spent the majority of the day feeling very ill indeed.

My family kept taking the mick out of me because of the cocktails, but I had only had three drinks and would have needed about ten to make me feel that bad! Over the course of the holiday, I began to notice that I felt really down; in fact, depressed. And I started to have strange and dark thoughts – I even began to imagine what I would write in my suicide letter. I was utterly beside myself. My throat was also hurting, so I could physically feel that pain within in my body alongside this deep depression.

When the suicidal thoughts persisted, I knew THIS IS NOT MINE. So, I decided to go for a walk by myself to clear this energy. I had already told my mum, who was back in England, that I was picking up on an energy that was not mine, and I asked her to be on hand to help clear this. I hadn't told my mum about the female I'd picked up at the start of my holiday, though.

By that stage, I had undergone a lot of both mediumship and energy removal training, so I was already doing clearings and spirit removal by myself. But due to the throat pain and how drained I felt, I wanted to have extra support with the clearing. After I released my part, my mum got in touch and said she had picked up the exact same as me. She had also picked up on the female in the corridor.

We both picked up that this lady had taken her own life because she was very lost and depressed, and after a bit of research we found out that there had been a female who used to work at the hotel that had taken her own life. She completely fitted the description of the lady I saw. Once she was released, the throat pain and the emotional side completely went, and I was able to continue my holiday in peace.

This was a huge turning point for me with my spiritual development and my career, because it really made me up my protection, but also helped me to understand just how much our energy can be affected by things like alcohol. Even if it's just one drink, if we are not putting out the right type of protection then our energy field will be lowered.

That lost lady did not mean to harm me intentionally; she most likely saw my light shining and knew somehow that I could help her, but unfortunately she ended up attaching slightly to my energy and drained me quite considerably. If I had not been aware of my own energy and my own thought process that I hold, I might have carried that for a lot longer and become very miserable, possibly ending up having prescribed medicine which I didn't really need. I could even have ended up seriously considering taking my own life, because her energy was mirrored onto mine. When you think about it like that, it's pretty bloody scary.

That is an example of taking on a spirit's characteristics. Because the spirit's emotions were strong, I began to act how she would have acted. The sensations I experienced were again more on the physical side, and the reactions linked to that would have been reacting emotionally to the thoughts I was hearing. I also reacted physically when my throat was sore.

Clairempathy exercise

I would like you to take your journal and pen and write down a time when you can remember experiencing an emotion or a physical pain that was not yours.

Can you recognise how it happened? When? And why? Are you able to remember how it triggered certain feeling and thoughts within you?

Did it perhaps even trigger any other senses like visuals, hearing etc?

Exercise two

Again, using your journal and pen, write down a list of people that you feel things around, then think about these questions:

How do you feel after you have been with that person? Do you feel drained or depressed/ tired? Perhaps you feel happy or excited?

Have you come away with any physical pains after seeing a particular person on your list? How long did it last for, or do you still feel it now?

Once you have written some things on your list, you will be able to see what is yours and what is not, from being with those people.

If you are around someone who you feel very drained by, this will indicate that you need to learn sufficient protection to help block or remove negative energy that does not serve your own energy. Please check protection techniques in Chapter 10.

Chapter 7

Claircognizance – Clear Knowing

Claircognizance: From the late 17th century French, *clair* ('clear') and *cognizance* ('knowing') The psychic ability of a person to acquire knowledge without knowing how they acquired it.

Have you ever had such a strong knowing that something was going to happen but had no explanation of how you knew? You just knew? And then it actually happened. Have you ever had such a strong knowing that someone was going to ring you, then they actually did? This is all a form of your claircognizance.

The clear knowing within us is very interesting, and we can receive it in a positive manner and a negative manner. This clear knowing sense is not a premonition – some people get this mixed up. Clear knowing is a sense within its own right, whereas a premonition is a form of internal clairvoyance (remember Chapter Two). However, as I always say, if you receive claircognizance it can trigger your other clairs to ignite, so you may well get the strong knowing which gives you more of an understanding due to the other clairs triggering.

Clear knowing is stronger than a sense; it's a very clear understanding of what is going to happen. Usually, when you get the clear knowing sense, it can kick in very strongly and can shock you – especially when something you knew then happens. Usually what we know tends to happen quite soon after – within minutes, hours, or a few days.

Claircognizance can feel great, too, as we don't tend to question it when it kicks in. However, we don't usually experience it all the time. You will most likely find that when you start to study your clairs and which ones are working more strongly for you, more of the other clairs will kick in. I think the reason we don't get clear knowing all the time is because we would start to get used to that strong knowing feeling and then maybe not recognise it as a sign. It's like with anything in life: when we are used to it, we don't seem to get the significance or impact of it as much.

Often people get clairsentient and claircognizance mixed up, but when you start to practise the different techniques throughout the book, you will notice a big difference between the two clairsenses. Clairsentient will be more subtle and it won't necessarily come straight into your head, whereas claircognizance will be a lot more noticeable. So, when you speak it, you will be more dominant with your words; you will say things like 'I JUST KNOW', rather then 'I THINK'.

Sometimes people can be scared of this sense, because when we are receiving something negative through clear knowing, it can worry us – like an accident or even a death happening to or around us, or to someone we love. However, we can also receive clear knowing in a positive way, and just because it might be negative or worrying, it's important to assess the other clairs that ignite once clear knowing has kicked in, as this may help to paint more of a picture of what will happen within the negative or positive experience.

Let me tell you about a claircognizance experience of my own...

I have had many times where my claircognizance has kicked in, but there is one I remember very clearly.

I had been feeling anxious all day, as if something bad was going to happen. My grandmother had been in a deep sleep for over a week, and although the doctors had been saying for a long time that she could pass away any day, months had gone by and she was still with us. As a family we had decided that what would be would be. If she was meant to be alone when she passed, then maybe that's how it was supposed to happen within her contract of life; likewise, if someone from the family was meant to be with her, we were putting all our trust in our angels to guide us to her.

On the 6th December, 2017, I had been feeling anxious all day and just couldn't shake off that feeling; it was like waiting for something bad to happen. I remember being on the phone to my partner, and as I walked through the kitchen I noticed one magpie outside my window. In that moment, my clear knowing kicked in so strongly, and I interrupted my partner to tell him that my grandma was going to die that night. He said, 'Are you sure, honey? Why, what have the doctors said?' I But I replied, 'No, the doctors haven't been in touch today. I just know she's going tonight.'

With that, I got off the phone and rang my mother who was with my grandma. Mum said she needed to go and get her M.O.T. sorted on her car but would then go straight back. I told her I thought she should stay, as I was concerned she would not be there when Grandma passed, but Mum was sure she would get back.

For the rest of the day, I felt on edge and desperately wanted to rush to get to Grandma's, but I had to wait for my partner to finish work so he could watch the kids. And I also had the feeling during that time that Grandma was still alive and wasn't going to pass until later on.

When my partner arrived home, I went straight over to my Grandma's. There is nothing like the feeling of going into a situation where someone is going to die in front of you. As I got into her room, I just knew this was it. I watched her breathing change so drastically; it was like she had been waiting for me to get there. Within ten minutes of me arriving, she had passed away.

I held her hand and said we would look after Mum and that she could go, then I watched her take her last breath. It was the most magical moment I've ever experienced. Of course, I was devastated, and I had tried to warn my mum, but unfortunately she felt Grandma still had time. However, my grandma passed the way she did according to her contract of life, and how she was meant to pass over was exactly right for her contract. I have been ever thankful that I was chosen to be there with her, and I am especially grateful for that strong claircognizance that alerted me to get my ass over there in time.

Those last ten minutes with her are moments I will never forget. Thank you, Grandma, for the constant guidance you still continue to give to me. I am ever grateful for your magic.

That night Grandma passed, she left part of her energy with me, because from that point on, my senses took an upgrade, and I became stronger and stronger within my mediumship. My grandma was always proud of my ability and it made sense why she passed in front of me, because I speak with spirit every day, so why not witness death? I get it now, and that was apart of my contract, too, for me to learn.

If I hadn't listened to my clear knowing that day, Grandma might have been on her own when she passed over. Bless her soul.

Claircognizance exercise...

Take your pen and paper and note down a time when you think you had clear knowing. Write down why you think it was clear knowing.

Once you have done that, see if you can recognise what other clairs were ignited from your clear knowing kicking in, and write them down. For example, were you then receiving clear seeing or clear hearing, empathy, etc?

Chapter 8

Clairalience – Clear Smelling

Clairalience: From late 17th century French, *clair* ('clear') + *alience* ('smelling')

With this particular clair, it can be received internally and externally. By that I mean that sometimes we can receive a smell that seems to be inside our nose to start with, or sometimes it will be externally outside of our body. For instance, within a certain room or building, there might just be a slight whiff of a smell and then it's gone.

It's important not to get clairalience mixed up with clairsentient; many people think clairsentience is the clear smelling sense because of the wording. This is really key for learning, because if you are getting them mixed up you will not be recognising key points in your sensory system and you will miss important messages. You will not be able to assess them correctly if you do not know the difference.

Clairalience can be received mostly from spirit around us, yet sometimes we can receive the smells of those that are still living even though they are not actually with us at that time. This may be a form of telepathy or even someone visiting using OBE (Out of Body Experience).

Clairalience is a brilliant clair because, although it is seen as one of the least common clairs within us, when it kicks in our clear smelling can ignite many of our other clairsenses. For example, if you smell a lovely floral perfume, straight away it will trigger perhaps a memory in the form of an internal clear seeing, which then triggers your clear emotion within you, which then makes you think of your lovely nanny who wore that fabulous floral perfume. Those that believe in this and are strengthening their senses will most likely know that their lovely nanny is actually with them in that moment, and be able to get what her message is or why she is visiting at that time. However, some may not realise that their beloved nanny's spirit is visiting them, even though they were aware of the memory they had and the emotion.

When we can strengthen each clair – even the least common ones – we have the opportunity to really assess what the messages are which enable us to move forward with our lives or to help others to move through something in life.

The clairalience smells are so interesting. I, for one, have smelt some very strong smells that have led to some interesting stories of spirit indeed.

Types of Smells

As with each sense, the smells we receive can be both pleasant and unpleasant – some can even be very concerning. It is important to assess how you are feeling when you receive these smells, because this will help you to understand if the spirit around you is positive or negative. For instance, you might receive a strong, stale smell, but this doesn't mean the spirit is a negative one. It could just indicate that this spirit, when alive, was once a hoarder and lived in a very musty, stagnant place, full of many things that held that type of smell. In fact, this spirit could well be a very kind person, so please make sure you assess correctly by what other clairsenses are triggering.

You often hear people talking of positive smells such as a loved one's favourite perfume or flower. Maybe they were a keen gardener and grew amazing rose bushes, and the smell of roses was always strong when you entered their home.

Perhaps someone might get the strong smell of tobacco, and it reminds them of their grandad; the feelings they have in that moment are positive and bring a flash of a memory which always makes them think of happy times from their childhood. So, although they might be a non-smoker and wouldn't usually like the smell of tobacco smoke, they don't mind when it occurs in the way of clairalience.

Likewise, it isn't always pleasant. We might notice a smell that reminds us of someone who wasn't very nice, so the smell itself could simply be fine, but if it's linked to bad memories it could well bring bad feelings or memories. Bear in mind that the spirit might not have the intention to bring a bad memory to us. They could simply be just visiting, but unfortunately whilst we are still earth-bound, we hold trauma within our energy, unless we take it upon ourselves to clear the negative memories or negative energy stuck within us.

Any smell you can think of will be on the list of clairalience smells, however these are some more of the common ones: flowers, perfume, tobacco, cigarettes, pipes, soaps, washing products, animal smells such as dogs or cats, fuel or oil, types of foods like sweets or cooking odours, musty stagnated smells, clean open spaces, hospital smells, TCP, certain types of medicine, burning, bad breath, bodily odours, disease – even the smell of death or dying is quite a common one.

So yes, some of those do not sound nice, but really, it's just another part of life. There are many other smells that can come through, too, but ultimately it all depends on what smell was lined to this spirit when they were alive and if that's the way they are going to start communication with you first. They may well hold a particular smell but want to communicate with you through another type of clair. That's why I always say it's so important to fully understand every single clair and to strengthen each one, even if you do not feel you have it within you. If you practise the techniques, you will be surprised what you can do.

You may also smell the scent of spirit that are not linked to you, as in family or friends passed over. You might pick up the scent of spirit that is perhaps stuck in a place or building. That's why when people go on ghost hunts in old buildings, they often notice smells, but the scent linked to spirit can also be in modern places and buildings, as spirit can become stuck at any stage – not just from centuries before.

Let me tell you about an experience I had with my clairalience...

Me and my mum had been called out to a house to check out what the activity was and whether it could be cleared. As I moved around one room in particular, I became very aware of the scent of urine, but urine that had been left and grown stronger. So, I checked my other senses to make sure this was indeed a stale urine smell. I asked if anyone else could smell it, but they couldn't.

The people in the house did not own any pets, and the carpets had been freshly put down not long before. They were clean people who looked after their home, so you knew it was not physically there. The fact that no-one else could smell it meant I knew that it was linked to a spirit that was still residing there. As this whiff came in stronger, it ignited my physical clairempathy, and I started to feel very weak within my body. With that, my clairvoyance internal clear seeing kicked in, and I saw an image of an old lady who was looking very disgruntled. Her hair was wild, and she was dressed in a stained vest and pants, and had a walking stick. This visual then ignited my clairsentience, which helped me to understand her personality.

Due to how I was feeling and what I was seeing, I knew that this little old lady was not mentally stable, was nearing the end of her life, and had possibly lost her awareness of hygiene and social skills, because she seemed very much in her own world. But why, you might wonder, would she still hold these traits if she was in spirit? Well, it was because she had not passed over properly, so even though her physical form was no longer alive, her spirit body that was within her physical had become stuck. So she was unable to receive release from the physical conditions that took place when she was physically alive, which meant she was still very much behaving and acting as she did when she was alive. I could tell that she must have been neglected by family for long periods of time, because otherwise she might have been helped in some way.

What was happening was that she was very much still residing in the house as if it was her own home, and she was becoming frustrated because she couldn't find her things. She couldn't find her cat, and she wanted the light on all the time, and when the new owners would turn it off, she would throw or knock things over. She would turn the oven on and leave it on, because that is the way she would behave when alive. But, naturally, the new owners were finding all this very distressing.

Now that we knew the full extent from that clairalience sense kicking in, we were able to guide her spirit body to the light and help her to pass over properly. We were then able to clear the remaining energy that had built up over time in the house, refresh it, and keep it fully safe for the new owners.

When we checked back one week later, all activity had stopped. A year down the line, there was still no activity and the couple were so relieved and happy within their home.

Reasons why spirits can get stuck...

There will be many reasons as to why spirit do not pass over properly, including:

1. Trauma within their life that has caused deep-rooted pain that was never healed.
2. If they had a sudden passing, they may not actually realise they are even dead.
3. Unfinished business with another loved one who still remains alive.
4. If they had a very traumatic death, like a murder or torture – this can sometimes mean they become stuck (not in all cases).
5. Not wanting to leave their loved ones – fragments of their spirit body can be created and remain stuck in the physical realm.
6. Chords from their energy/spirit body to another who remains alive.
7. They may become very scared of passing, so they do not pass over properly due to fear of what is on the other side.
8. If they followed a particular religion or belief which held the theory of nothing after death, or a belief that you will be punished because you were feeling guilty of something in life, this can cause spirit to become stuck.

There are many different levels to this, and many different ways in which spirit can be assisted in fully returning to the light. This is why I always make sure that I approach every spirit – whether stuck or not – with the utmost respect, even if they are nasty or grumpy, etc. Every soul deserves to cross over properly, and they deserve that chance of healing and release.

Chapter 9

Clairgustance – Clear Tasting

Clairgustance: From 17th-century French, *clair* ('clear') + *gustance* ('taste')
The ability to taste a substance without putting anything in one's mouth. It is claimed that those who possess this ability are able to perceive the essence of a substance from the spiritual or ethereal realm through taste.

Aww, the fabulous clairgustance sense. Oh, I have had many experiences with this sense. Similar to clairalience, this clair is one of the least common senses that one holds within them, however it's a brilliant one because it triggers all of the other clairs off. So it will create a ripple effect of senses that allows you to understand what the message is.

Clairgustance will be predominantly mediumship-based, however there have been cases where people think the taste sense is working on more of a psychic energetic level.

Clear taste can be extremely interesting when it happens, or it can be quite disgusting, depending on what type of taste you are receiving. Absolutely any type of taste you can possibly imagine will come under the clairgustance sense, from the nice to the nasty. These will usually be linked in some way to the spirit who is communicating with you, whether that be something they used to eat a lot of, or perhaps smoked, or even a taste they experienced whilst dying. Perhaps they had to have regular medication and that taste of the medication stuck with them, so it could be something that comes through the clairgustance sense. Perhaps a great grandfather would chew tobacco and that is what you are tasting, even though you are not a known smoker.

Spirit will not mean to give you nasty tastes, so if the taste alarms you it will hopefully only be for a short while. If you know how to do your clair checks, you might be able to release the taste quicker than if you were not aware of your senses. It can act similar to clairempathy where the taste will hang around or keep happening until you register or understand the connection of the spirit.

If you receive a particular taste, it will trigger another clair, which will then unfold part of the story of who this spirit is. So your senses will be telling you what type of person they were, or what possibly happened to them, through feelings, hearing, visuals, sensing, smell, taste, etc.

Clairgustance can happen when a loved one of your own is around you wanting to connect, or even when there are complete stranger spirits that have no link to you at all. Again, these can be nice or possibly nasty spirits, but it's important to remember that a bad taste in your mouth does not mean this is necessarily a bad spirit.

Let me tell you about an experience I had with clairgustance...

I was sitting doing a reading with a client and had been connecting to some loved ones of hers when I became aware of a strong taste of very sour torte berries in my mouth. It was so sour it made me shake with quite a strong reaction, and my eyes started to water. Because I was already in reading mode, I knew straight away this was from spirit. However, I wasn't getting it beforehand, when I was connecting to this lady's dad, so I knew that a new energy of a different spirit had stepped in to communicate. With that taste I instantly got the clairsentience kick in, and I sensed this was an older female. This then ignited my clairvoyance internal clear seeing, and I started to see in my mind what this older female looked like. She was quite a rosy-cheeked, plump lady, wearing an apron, and had shoulder-length, white, curly, fluffy hair. I could then feel her personality, which was fun, loud, and friendly, but knew she was also a firm and traditional homemaker and clearly loved to cook.

From that original taste, she then took me on a journey, showing me how she would take this lady who was having the reading, through the fields and down to the hedges to pick the small berries for her pies. This triggered my clairempathy emotional, because I suddenly felt really loving and wanted to cry with joy at how much she loved doing this with the sitter, who was actually her granddaughter. She showed me that when they would get home from collecting the berries, they would try to eat a few before she stewed them, and they would always have this same reaction I'd had because of how sour they were.

The lady having the reading was crying because she just loved that this memory had been described to her in so much detail, and she could see my reaction to the taste was exactly the same as theirs when she was young. It brought her so much joy hearing that memory and it also brought her evidence so that she could trust and know 100% that this was her grandmother talking to us.

So, you can see that from just that initial taste kicking in I was able to receive a huge amount of significance.

Just think about what we miss when we don't tap in and assess exactly what we are receiving. The more we become aware of each sense, the more we can piece them together and strengthen them. All it takes is acceptance, awareness, practice, and assessment.

There will be moments in our spiritual development that we will never forget, from the very simple all the way to the extreme ones that almost seem unreal. However, we will remember the moments that brought real significance either to ourselves or to others. Every day is about learning.

I am a working medium, but I still see every single session I do as a chance to develop and move forward. There are always areas we can access further. Who wouldn't want to do this? It's an amazing process, and connecting and developing your clairs will only make you a more varied, more in-depth, and more in-tune, stronger person within your spiritual and your practical life.

Clairgustance exercise

Take your pen and paper and write down any times you can remember when you received a particular taste in your mouth. Write down how you became aware of it and how it made you feel.

- Were you able to recognise the taste was not yours?
- What were the senses that were triggered next?
- How long or how often did this taste occur? For instance, was it after someone's passing? Or perhaps when you lived in a particular place, so it stopped when you left there?
- Was there a pattern to it? Would it occur at the same time every day or week?
- Were you able to understand the message? Or did you always wonder what that could have been?
- When you have written all of those down, you will already start to understand what it was that happened, even if you didn't realise it at the time.

Chapter 10

Spiritual Protection

So, you have probably been reading all about the clairs and wondering how to protect yourself when some of these clairs kick in and give you very strong experiences. Of course, you will also be thinking about the different ways to protect yourself when doing different types of spiritual development, whether connecting psychically or in a mediumistic way.

There are so many different techniques to protect ourselves. It is important to remember, though, that as we move through the motions of our spiritual upgrades, we must also make sure we are balancing out our protection to match what we receive.

When thinking about our protection, it is also important to be aware of our thought patterns and how we perceive protection. When I say this, I simply mean that sometimes we can be doing protection yet still feel unsafe or unprotected. Or perhaps we think that we are protected so we don't need to do protection. Really, this is individual to however you choose to think.

When I was younger, I would have a lot of contact from spirit or energies, some of which made me feel uncomfortable, on edge, or scared, so I would often tell myself I was unprotected. This was something I chose to believe, which in a sense made the feeling stronger. So, I started to learn many different protection techniques, and this is when I began to understand the impact of my beliefs around my protection. This then led me on a journey to discover how to let go of these limiting beliefs and also how to feel protection strongly within my energy.

The stronger my mediumistic senses became, the more I realised I needed to change up my protection to match the energy frequency of my senses. Perhaps the previous protection techniques I had been regularly doing needed upgrading too, or tweaking. This is why I often say to my students that it's important to go with the flow when doing protection or any spiritual exercise. Of course, you should follow the steps or guidance which you already know, but if you are feeling drawn to focus on something new coming into your mind during your spiritual exercise, then you must listen to this feeling because it will be guidance from your angels. As long as you always remain to have the intention of receiving protection, you will be fine.

Protection Techniques

Here are some simple techniques that you can try. You can expand on these techniques whenever you feel you want to. I would recommend trying out a few different ones from of this list, to see which ones suit you the best.

Protection Technique One

Make sure you have five to ten minutes in a quiet environment where you will not be interrupted.

1. Sit quietly with your eyes shut.
2. Take some deep breaths in, allowing your body to become more relaxed as you exhale out.
3. On the third deep breath, hold this breath for the count of three, and as you exhale begin to imagine pure white light starting to cascade all around you. (Don't worry if you do not see the white light, just the thought will be strong enough. So, please don't think it's not working if you don't visualise.)
4. As you hold yourself in the space of pure white light, begin to imagine this white light energy starting to form a beautiful big bubble around you.
5. Focus on watching or imagining your whole body standing inside this bubble, and make sure you focus on drawing this white light bubble completely around you.
6. Spend a while checking that there are no gaps or holes in this bubble. If you feel there are gaps/holes, draw the energy of the bubble around to close them.
7. As you focus on your bubble, start to visualise or think about the bubble vibrating and radiating out that beautiful white light.
8. Then imagine that any external energy – whether neutral or negative – cannot get through this bubble.
9. Know that this is your protection.
10. Say in your mind 'Positive in and out only', and repeat a few times

11. Give thanks for your protection.

This is a really simple technique that you can expand upon or use different colours. You can spend as much or as little time as you want to do this. I like to practise seeing the vibrations coming off the bubble and watching the energy pulse out.

Protection Technique Two

Make sure you have five to ten minutes in a quiet comfortable environment, where you will not be interrupted.

1. Close your eyes and begin to take some deep breaths, allowing your body to become more and more relaxed.
2. After three or four nice deep breaths, as you exhale imagine that you are standing in the space of white light.
3. Focus on that white light, drawing it stronger into your mind.
4. Focusing now on your crown chakra, imagine beautiful golden energy being pulled from the left of your crown chakra and down, all the way round the left side of your body, under your feet, and back up round the right side of your body, and that golden energy attaching to the right side of your crown chakra.
5. See that ring of golden light ignite as it attaches to your crown chakra.
6. Now imagine that you are pulling golden light from the front of your golden chakra, down around the front

of your body again, all the way under your feet, and up round the back of your body, focusing on it attaching to the back of your crown chakra.

7. As it attaches to the back of the crown, imagine that ring of golden light ignite.
8. You will now be aware of two golden halos crossing over under your feet and over the top of your head.
9. Focusing on this golden cross of halos, now draw the golden energy and stretch the energy from each halo to create a beautiful golden bubble all around you.
10. Know that this is your protection, and imagine any negative energies now being blocked from being able to get through this golden bubble.
11. Speak out your gratitude for your protection.

You can expand upon this technique as much as you wish to. Again, I like to imagine the golden halos vibrating and that energy protecting me.

Protection Technique Three

Make sure you have five to ten minutes in a quiet environment with no interruptions.

1. With your eyes closed, begin to take some deep breaths.
2. As you take these deep breaths, let your body become more and more relaxed.
3. With your third deep breath, hold this for three counts, and as you exhale begin to imagine an invisible energy field starting to wrap around you in the shape of a box.

4. As you imagine this box, imagine you can see yourself in this box.
5. Focus on the strength of the protection from these energy fields.
6. Now imagine that your angel is presenting you with an angelic testing tool – one which they will use to gently throw at these energy fields around you.
7. Perhaps you see angelic hammers, spiritual rocks, maybe golden swords. These tools are not designed to hurt you; they are merely to help you to test your protection field.
8. As you imagine these angelic tools lovingly being thrown towards your protection fields, you will become aware of whether they burst, or create slits or holes within your protection field. If they don't, then you will know that your protection is sufficient. However, if they do get through, this will be a loving test from your angels to go back and reaffirm your protection until there are no more gaps/slits or holes.
9. Then, when you are happy that your protection field is fully complete and secure, start to radiate light through the energy box you are in.
10. This energy field box will keep out negative energies.

I like to do this one when I feel I need extra support from negative people or spirit. The more you practise this technique, the better you will become at understanding fully whether you need to reaffirm your protection. It will become easier for you to understand your energy and whether something feels fully complete the more you practice assessing how your energy fields or bubbles are working for you.

These are just three examples you can try, but there are many other types of protection techniques. I share many of my techniques over at my membership The School of Spirituality, which offers many spiritual aspects.

Chapter 11

Grounding

Some of you may be aware of grounding and its importance. Some of you may practise it and others may have never tried it.

For me, grounding is something that has proved to be extremely important within my spiritual journey. I went from never doing it, to doing it every single day.

What is grounding?

Grounding is a way in which we channel our energy and connect ourselves to the elements of Mother Earth, and brings physical and emotional balance and strength. When you learn how to ground yourself, you become so much more present in your body, emotions, spirituality, and energy. You find that you have less drama or upsetting things occur in your life, or that you are able to deal and understand with challenging issues. Grounding helps you to become strong within all areas of your life.

Grounding can help with both our physical energy and our spiritual energy, and can also help towards spiritual protection. However, it is not full protection.

It's especially important to ground yourself when doing any form of mediumship or channelling/trance, etc, because you will be working with the light or source energy which can sometimes become very intense or make you feel floaty. And while that can feel lovely, it does not help our physical form to function in day-to-day life. So being grounded can help to keep us level and balanced with our physical form.

Most people like to ground themselves in a quiet, meditative way. However, it's important to remember that grounding is not a meditation. It can be tagged onto the start or end of a meditation, but if you are not connecting to the earth within a meditation, then you will not have had grounding.

There are many ways to ground yourself and many aspects and things to do that can naturally help ground yourself – some do not require doing the relaxed techniques.

Here are ten tips to follow to ensure that you are bringing that grounded energy you need to yourself outside of doing meditative grounding:

1. **Food and water**

   When you eat and drink, you are physically brought closer to Mother Earth. Water is cleansing and helps to flush out any energy that is not serving you, and certain foods give you the energy you need to remain stable within the physical form and the physical realm.

2. **Exercise**

   You can put your physical and your mind in a good

state by exercising. No matter what activity you choose, whether it be light exercise or a more vigorous workout, your body will receive more positive energy and naturally feel more grounded. By exercising you will better understand your body and energy, and will feel when you need grounding.

3. **Nature**

   Spending more time in nature, immersing yourself amongst the trees, is a great way of grounding. Standing barefoot on the grass, or rock, stone, sand, wood – whatever land, as long as its natural – is a brilliant way of connecting your physical energy to Mother Earth's energy. If you make a conscious effort to disconnect from distractions in everyday life, from those around you, traffic, your phone, etc, then you will find you have the time to assess what is in your way and you mind will become clearer. Whether you are walking in mountains, or along a beautiful beach, lying on the grass, or sitting on a big rock, you are giving yourself the time to receive the grounded energy from the earth. Another brilliant way of using nature is to keep lots of plants in your home or in a lovely spiritual room, and let their energy soak into your energy.

4. **Salt Baths**

   Having a fabulous salt bath, with Epsom salts or Himalayan salt, is a great way to ground yourself – again with the cleansing of the water. Salt is also an amazing way to protect yourself. Not only will it help your skin, but the energy from these natural salts of the earth will help to release negative energy as you learn to ground yourself spiritually.

5. **Eat Dark Chocolate**
   Some of you may be thinking that chocolate is unhealthy – yes, most chocolate is – but raw, dark or organic chocolate is fabulous for grounding yourself, and the purer the chocolate the more you can use its energy to ground yourself. Don't forget, pure cocoa comes from the cacao tree, which is of the land, therefore it brings plenty of grounding. If you manage to find salted dark chocolate, this is also great as you have a mix of the two grounding aspects. The chocolate helps to ground your physical form.

   I always take organic dark salted chocolate with me when I go to big psychic events or even house clearings, because I want to keep my grounded energy up in a busy environment with many other energies around.

6. **Crystals**
   Using crystals to help ground yourself is a brilliant way to become more connected to your body and to the earth. Of course, crystals are of the earth and hold many properties that are beneficial, alongside grounding energies. Trying techniques with crystals to ground yourself is a good idea, as well as wearing crystals as a necklace or somewhere on you. Red jasper, tiger's eye, septarian, and smoky quartz are all brilliant for grounding, and there are many others. Make sure you research the meanings of the crystals, but also be

aware if you are drawn to particular crystals, as they will be the ones which your energy needs most at that time.

7. **Assess Your Signs**
   You must start becoming aware of the signs which your body shows you when you are ungrounded. Learning to spot these signs is vital and you should make a point of checking yourself regularly. If you experience dizziness, shakiness, forgetfulness, excessive daydreaming, feeling un-present, you can use the necessary techniques to draw your energy back to the earth and to your body.

8. **Meditation**
   This is a fabulous way to practise grounding, As I explained earlier, you can do grounding within a meditation, but you must connect your roots to the earth in order for it to be grounding. So, it is down to the individual if they want to do just a grounding visualisation, or if they then want to go into a journey within the meditation. Some also like to do grounding after a meditation, and it can take as long or as little time as you like.

   I always say to my students, you must make sure that when you are connecting your roots that you practise different ways. For instance, some like to imagine roots from their feet; some like to work on their root chakra and imagine the root chakra energy moving down to the earth; some even like to imagine roots from the base of their spine moving downwards into the earth; some like to do grounding first before protection.

I would recommend you do grounding first, then protection, and then go about your day or the spiritual activity that you want to do.

9. Using Heavy Natural Objects

This is another great grounding tip. You might feel silly trying it, but actually it really helps you to feel that lovely, heavy, grounded energy. Get a sack of potatoes or some large, heavy rocks, and sit quietly with them placed upon your feet, then just assess how it feels gently cementing your feet to the ground. This can really help, and is good to try whilst you are doing a visualisation of your roots connecting.

10. Other People

Whilst doing your grounding visualisation, sometimes it helps to have someone else who you trust to gently hold your feet for a short while. This person must have the intention to help ground you lovingly and authentically. Some may like this technique, while others might not want to try it; it depends how you feel about other people and the energy they hold. If you are like the way I used to be, you might be worried about the transfer of other people's energy to you. After years of practising and trusting my protection, I now do not mind other people touching me, but I went through a stage where I did not want anyone to touch me – not even to shake my hand or cuddle me – because I felt so weary of picking up others energy. However, this was down to my belief pattern I had around protection. Once I truly believed that my protection worked, I was able to trust others more and trust others' energy around me.

Grounding Visualisations

There are so many amazing ways to ground yourself in a meditative state. The title says visualisation, but don't be put off if you don't see during visualisation. Just hearing the words, if you're listening to grounding guidance, or the mere thoughts within your mind, will be just as strong to help you be grounded.

Here are some great grounding techniques to try. You can expand upon these techniques any time you want, and make them longer or shorter according to your energy or what you want to do with your experience. It's important to try out lots of different grounding techniques so you can find what works best for you.

Remember that the more spiritual upgrades you have the more you will need to focus on your grounding. And make sure your grounding is balanced with the spiritual energy frequency you are at along your spiritual journey.

Grounding Technique One

Mother Earth Crystal Grounding

Take these simple steps to guide yourself into grounding.

Make sure you have five to ten minutes to sit quietly in a safe environment where you will not be interrupted.

1. Sit quietly with your eyes closed and begin to take some nice deep breaths.
2. Concentrating on your deep breaths, let your body become more and more relaxed.
3. On your third or fourth deep breath, start to imagine roots coming from the soles of your feet. As you imagine these roots, see them growing through each layer of Mother Earth
4. Zoom in on your roots and check out the texture of them; can you see or feel the colour of your roots?
5. Make sure you focus on your roots round the back of you, underneath the ground.
6. Focus on soaking up the beautiful, loving, grounded energy from Mother Earth.
7. As you imagine your roots, think about how they grow: Do they grow long and thin, windy, or are they very chunky? Let them grow exactly how they need to each day for you.
8. Now focus on your special roots drawing closer to a big chunk of crystal under the ground; any crystal you think of will be right for you on each day you do it. As your roots get closer, watch or imagine your roots connecting to this crystal.
9. As they connect, see your roots becoming ignited with the beautiful crystal energy.
10. Begin to focus on this crystal energy now travelling back up through your roots. Concentrate on feeling or seeing this energy pulsing up through each layer of Mother Earth that your roots grew through.
11. Eventually this crystal energy, along with the grounded energy of Mother Earth begins to enter the soles of your feet.

12. As this energy enters your feet, imagine that your roots are growing through the top of your feet and wrapping around them. Feel these roots firmly but gently cementing you to the ground.
13. As you focus on this, think about it drawing up your legs.
14. This is where you can go on into a meditation or, if you don't want to do a meditation, you can continue to do whatever protection you choose. Or, if you feel ready, you can begin to wiggle your feet, stretch your legs and body, and bring your awareness fully back into your physical form and the room.
15. When you are fully back to your normal state, make sure you drink some filtered water.

Grounding Technique Two

Land/Waterpool Grounding

Make sure you have five to ten minutes to sit quietly in a safe environment where you will not be interrupted.

1. Sit quietly with your eyes closed and begin to take some nice deep breaths.
2. Concentrating on your deep breaths, let your body become more and more relaxed.
3. On your third or fourth deep breath, start to focus on visualising or thinking of your bare feet and imagine what type of land you are standing on. Maybe it's a nice slab of crystal or a lovely grassy patch, perhaps a nice smooth pebble or even warm sand.

4. As you think about this land, begin to imagine that this land is vibrating. As it vibrates, see or feel the energy of the vibrations starting to tingle around your feet.
5. As you continue to feel this land vibrating, imagine that your feet are gently becoming immersed under this land that you stood on. The ground is gently soaking your feet with loving, warm energy.
6. Now imagine that your feet are safely tucked under this ground, and the ground is firmly and warmly cemented around your ankles.
7. As you now focus on your feet being underground, start to imagine those roots of yours drawing out of your feet and breaking through each layer of Mother Earth.
8. As your roots grow deeper and deeper underground, make sure you have a good look at the colour and texture of your roots.
9. Continue to focus on your roots moving through the earth, and think about the goodness of the ground entering your roots. As your roots draw deeper, start to become aware of a lovely pool of precious water deep underground.
10. This lovely pool of water calls in your roots, and you focus on them now soaking up this cleansing water.
11. Imagine now that this water is being soaked back up through your roots, through each layer of Mother Earth.
12. Eventually, this lovely cleansing water is now starting to approach and enter the soles of your feet.
13. As this cleansing water and the grounded energy of Mother Earth soak up through your feet, you can now

feel that splendid energy starting to merge up through your body.

14. Say in your mind: 'This is my grounding. Thank you. Thank you. Thank you.'
15. This is where you can then begin a journey meditation, or if you prefer, you can go on to do your protection.
16. If you wish to do neither, this is where you will now begin to wiggle your feet and stretch your legs, taking a deep breath to bring your awareness back into the room.
17. Now please make sure you drink some filtered water to help with this grounding.

TOP TIP

Make sure when focusing on your roots that you also imagine the roots round the back of you, underneath the ground, as many people mainly focus on straight down underneath and to the front. It is very important to practise focusing on the back, too.

TOP TIP TWO

When we imagine the colour and texture of our roots, this can really help to make us feel extra grounded, because we are studying in more depth what our roots look like. That thought process of focusing on it brings the intention of grounding to us more strongly.

Grounding Technique Three

Base Chakra Grounding

Make sure you have five to ten minutes to sit quietly in a safe environment where you will not be interrupted.

1. Sit quietly with your eyes closed, taking some deep breaths.
2. Let your body become more and more relaxed as you exhale.
3. On your third or fourth deep breath, hold this for the count of three, then exhale.
4. As you exhale, let your awareness guide you to your root/base chakra down by the base of your spine, and start to imagine that deep burgundy colour of your base now becoming brighter and brighter.
5. Let this beautiful burgundy colour start to swirl round and round within your base chakra.
6. As it does, imagine your beautiful, unique roots now starting to grow out of the base of your spine and gently forming down around your legs, around the front and the back.
7. Imagine these roots now starting to enter into the ground, and begin to focus on them roots breaking through each layer of Mother Earth.
8. Have a good look at or think about the colour and texture of these roots as they are growing deeper and deeper underground.
9. Know in your mind that your roots are starting to soak up the loving grounded energy that you need from Gaia.

10. Now focus on Gaia's energy starting to pulse back up through these special roots of yours. Imagine the energy is now starting to enter into the soles of your feet and that you are receiving the grounding that you need.
11. Focus on this energy now travelling back up through your roots that are wrapped around your legs. This grounded energy is now connecting to your root/base chakra mixing with that beautiful burgundy colour.
12. Say in your mind: 'This is my grounding. Thank you. Thank you. Thank you.'
13. Here you can now go into meditation or continue on to your protection.
14. When ready, you can now wiggle your feet, taking a nice deep breath and stretching your legs, bringing your awareness back into the room.
15. Make sure you have a drink of filtered water.

TOP TIP

When focusing on the root/base chakra, if you are unsure of the chakras or where they are positioned within your energy stream, then please do research m. Some people like to do a chakra balance through all the chakra energy points, and then continue to do the root/base grounding. It depends how long you want to spend on the grounding technique. However, if you choose not to do the chakra balance beforehand, it will still work well just focusing on the base chakra.

Grounding Technique Four

Your Special Tree Grounding

Make sure you have five to ten minutes to sit quietly in a safe environment where you will not be interrupted.

1. Sit quietly with your eyes closed and begin to take some nice deep breaths.
2. As you take your deep breaths, allow your body to become more and more relaxed.
3. With your third deep breath, hold this one for the count of three and allow yourself to imagine that you are looking at your bare feet.
4. As you see your feet, start to imagine that some huge tree trunks are starting to form from your feet.
5. As these tree trunks form, you realise that they are your roots. Focus on them growing deep into the ground.
6. Imagine these roots soaking up all the grounded energy that you need to get on with your day and to help make you feel strong.
7. As this energy from the earth starts to pump back up through these beautiful tree trunk roots, imagine that this energy is entering back up through your feet and up your legs.
8. Imagine that your legs are now lovingly being wrapped with beautiful bark, and that a lovely big tree is starting to form all around you. You will see or think about your body being inside the tree.
9. As you continue to focus on this tree, imagine or visualise the leaves and branches now starting to form

with the leaves beautifully cascading down to create lovely warmth and protection.

10. Imagine you have a bird's eye view of yourself; think or see how the tree looks with yourself lovingly inside it.
11. Now imagine that this tree is igniting, switching on your grounding and protection fully, ready for your day.
12. Say: 'This is my grounding. Thank you. Thank you. Thank you.'
13. Here is where you can continue into a meditation or onto more protection.
14. When you are ready, you can now start to wiggle your feet, taking a nice deep breath, stretching your legs and bringing your awareness back into the room.
15. Have a glass of filtered water.

TOP TIP

Make sure you allow whatever tree you think, see, or feel, to come in. It can be as big or small as you like. Practise focusing on the texture of the bark and the leaves, and noticing all those beautiful colours. Always give thanks for your grounding.

Chapter 12

Elly's Spiritual Must-Know Meanings List

It is so important to know the true meanings of the spiritual aspects of life. I meet so many who are knowing of parts of their spirituality and how it's working for them, but there are so many pieces to the puzzle that are missing within their understanding – including many of the basics. This does not in any way mean they are stupid. It simply means that maybe they never had somebody to fully guide them and explain what each meaning is. There are so many that perhaps they didn't always think to ask.

I have put together a MUST-KNOW list that I feel includes the really key elements to our natural spiritual growth. Please go through the meanings or check back with this list should you come across any of them.

Of course, this book is all about our clairsensory system, so we will gain a great deal of in-depth knowledge about each of those clairs. However, it is so important to understand other aspects, like the difference between psychism and mediumship, and how our clairs can tap into both of those sources as well as our practical and physical energies.

Akashic Records – Akasha means SKY or SPACE, and it's said to be a collection of mystical knowledge that is stored away in a non-physical plane of existence. Akashic records are said to have existed since the beginning of existence, and include human, animal, and land energy. So, our soul contracts have a lot to do with delving into the akashic records and delving into many past and future lives. The reason why some are so interested in working through the akasha energy will be to find out what their soul work was previously, and how that energy can help in this life, including after-life experiences. This is another reason why people are drawn to OBEs.

Attachments – Attachments come in all shapes and forms, from spirit, to energy, to stuck trauma, to a thought pattern. Attachments can also be brought forward from past lives, or chords that have been sent out to you from another. Psychic attack is also a type of attachment. Not all attachments are negative; there could be attachments linked to some lovely people or lovely spirit. But if it is not your energy, then over time this will not serve you, no matter how nice they were. If, for instance, there is a spirit attachment, there are many different levels of spirit. The most common is lost souls, which are usually innocent and do not mean to attach themselves to you. There are a number of reasons why they will attach: 1. Because they are unaware that they are dead; 2. Because they are hoping you can help them; 3. Because they find something in you that is similar to themselves; 4. Because maybe they didn't want to leave you, or you didn't want them to go – this one usually only links in to those that we had a good bond with;

it won't be a random spirit that we do not know.

How we remove an attachment can depend on how many there are, the level of the attachment – as in what type – and what avenue we use to remove it. This could be through healing, chord cutting, past life regression, energy removal, guiding spirit to the light, and many more. Attachment removal should be done by someone who is highly experienced. This person should also have high mediumship connection, so that if it is a spirit attachment, they are able to connect to that soul properly and help guide them to the light.

Divination – The use of tools to give readings. Such as tarot cards, tea leaf readings, palm reading, pendulums, crystals, ogham staves, runes, ribbons, etc.

Mediumship – This is purely connection with spirit, whether it be your own loved ones, your ancestors, someone else's loved ones, or even spirit that is possibly stuck between the physical and spirit realms. A medium will then, using their clairs, access who this spirit is and what the messages are, if any, to pass on.

Mental Medium/ mental Mediumship – This is someone who has progressed through their mediumship journey connecting to spirit in a very safe and protected way, understanding fully how their clairsensory system works within them, and understanding how to close down after spirit connection. A mental medium will also choose when they connect to spirit and if they want to talk to each spirit attempting to connect. This means they have learned what type of grounding and protection works well for them, and are actively working on their spiritual wellbeing. So, if spirit does connect, they already know and are prepared because they chose for it to happen and when the connection ends.

OBE – Out of Body Experience or Astral Travel – This is where our spirit body will leave our physical body for a period of time, and may occur in our sleep or whilst we are awake. It could be uncontrolled, or it might be done on purpose. Those, like myself, who practise this in a purposeful manner will usually do OBEs to better their understanding of: 1. Energy; 2. The spirit world; 3. To gain spiritual knowledge; 4. To even visit their loved ones passed over. If done safely and correctly, it can be life-changing and better your awareness of who you are as an individual, but also how to use the spiritual realm to help others.

Partial Projection – This is where parts of your spirit body will be projecting out of your physical body, which will mean that your spirit body is starting an OBE. This does not mean that you will 100% go out of your body; sometimes it happens, and sometimes it doesn't. It all depends on whether someone is doing this on purpose to deliberately get out of their body or whether they are actually unaware. These areas where partially projected will usually feel heavy and numb, or the person will have lost awareness of the physical part. So, sometimes when you are nodding off and your body twitches, this will actually be your spirit body shifting.

Psychism – The means of using your energy to tune into someone else's energy who is alive, to give guidance on past, present, and future situations.

Psychic Attack – As mentioned earlier, psychic attack is a form of attachment, and can be mild to extreme. This happens when someone is sending energy out to another person in a negative way, which this person will over time start to feel. Whether they realise what it is or not, it's a very manipulative energy, as in the sense that it might not be recognised for a while as it will impact someone in ways which a person can put down to logical circumstance, for example, feeling drained, getting ill, or just plain bad luck.

As I said, there are different levels to psychic attack, and some do not intentionally mean to send it out and would probably not want to make another ill. However, some do intentionally want to harm others by sending negative thoughts and energy to them. A major cause of psychic attack is usually jealousy, or wanting to control someone or something. Psychic attack can harm you, and I have been through this myself in my younger days. I experienced that negative energy towards me, so I know how harmful it can be. However, when it comes to psychic attack, it has a lot to do with your belief system; if you believe that their negative energy will harm you in some way, then it will.

Once I did a lot of work on changing my mindset around this, I was able to move forward, knowing that others' negative energy couldn't hurt me any more if I believed it had no power. There are also psychic energetic actions that can be taken to release psychic attack from someone, through a loving means, of course.

Another form of psychic attack will be from spirit to human. This will happen in a different way and is not usually to do with jealousy. It's normally because you are maybe running your energy in a lower vibrational frequency, so there will be a tendency to have lower energy spirit around you who will want to reside within part of your energy. Or it could be because you are doing light work, and those spirits want to keep you from your light work because they want to control with a darker power. Again, the impact of this can be very similar to the other forms of psychic attack, so you can get poorly, feel very drained and unmotivated to do positive things or light work, etc. This can be cleared by working with an experienced medium.

Psychometry – This involves using an object that belongs to someone who passed over, to connect with their spirit. Another way of using objects will be for those who are still alive. So, a psychic might wish to hold a lady's engagement ring that was brand new and only belonged to her, and pick up on the energy within the object to give guidance on the lady's life currently.

Another form of psychometry is using photographs. Again, you can look at an image of someone who has passed over and connect to their spirit, using your clairs to then assess who they are and what they would like to tell you. Or you can use an image of someone who is alive and tap in psychically to give them guidance. It is very interesting working with images, especially if they were taken when someone was going through real key moments, either positive or negative. You must remember, though, that if someone gives you an image from a year ago or even ten years ago, you might pick up a lot more about their past than the present. So, if someone wants guidance for their present or future, you must ask them to provide an up-to-date image. Or you can use your clairs to assess what is coming up in their future.

Source – This can be expressed in which way you feel most connected to view it. Source simply means the connection to your spiritual energy from a higher means. Some think of source as love; some think of it as the white light; some think of source as energy, the creator, heaven, the spirit realm, angelic realm, etc. But really, source is everything, so you can believe in whatever you want to when you think of source. What I would say is to trust what comes through when you connect to source, because this will guide you into who your spirit guides are, and what type of energy is within you, around you, and coming to you at a later date.

Soul Contracts – Our soul is pure energy that moves through lives as and when our soul is assigned to do so. Our soul knows the depth of who we are and what we will become, including the challenges that we will face in each life. Our soul will allow us to learn the lessons that were written into our contract for each life, and our contracts will hold our purpose to each life. That is why we will have premonitions or déjà vu, because we are being given snippets of our future.

When you have readings, and psychics or mediums give you predictions around your future and then it comes true, that is because they are accessing parts of your contract. Nothing is a coincidence; everything is written, whether positive or negative. Our loved ones who pass over can sometimes be shown our contracts and they can then act as guides for us, because they know at exactly every given moment what is coming up for our soul contract. Our guides will be highly respectful of our contract, though, and will not try to influence or change it. So, they will know exactly when we are going to struggle or if we are not going to listen to their guidance; likewise, they will know exactly when we are going to listen and what actions we will take. This will usually feel like we are receiving some great significance to act upon, or we will feel that we are divinely guided. Our soul also knows what is coming up, and part of the soul's journey is to let itself be discovered in an even more magnetic and powerful way than the last life it was in.

Submissive Medium – This means someone who is aware of a connection to spirit but is not in control of it, therefore they are submissive to the energies coming in. This usually happens when people are at the start of their spiritual journey and need to train. This can be exciting and interesting, but it could also be draining or even scary for the person if they are unaware spirit is there and then suddenly receive something. It means that they have most likely not done any protection or grounding beforehand so might not be able to let go of the messages or even physical sensations that the spirit has put upon them.

Spirit Guide Signature – This is usually done during a meditation to anchor in a sign from your spirit guide so that you know which one is connecting to you. Their signature will be locked in and you will usually receive this particular sign – for instance, a signature could be a colour, a word, a symbol, a pattern, a feeling. This signature can come into your mind as a visual or a thought, or you may hear or feel it. And you can receive an individual one for each spirit guide, whether they are a loved one you physically knew, an ancestor, an angel or ascended master, or perhaps even an animal guide. So, if you enhance your clairsensory, your connection with your guides will become stronger and clearer.

The more you practise receiving and locking in signatures, the more you will be able to detect when a new guide is coming to work with you and if you will understanding better whether this guide is of the light or of the dark.

TOP TIP

If you are feeling strange about a new guide that is around you, get yourself into a relaxed space and quiet your mind, with eyes shut and say:

Are you of the light?
Are you of the light?
Are you of the light?

Say this three times, and if they remain there with you, then you know they are genuine. If they resist this three-step process and disappear, then you know they were not genuine and most likely had ulterior motives for you. It so important to assess your guides correctly. Of course, if it's someone who has passed over that you knew and had a great bond with, you will already know that energy is safe. But if you ever feel unsure, check if they are of the light.

(If you're wondering what my sign is, check out my next chapter on The Sunflower Signature.)

Transition – This can mean a few things, so it will depend what context you are working in as to which one it means. Firstly, the obvious one is death – when someone is transitioning from the physical body into the spirit body, and what process they are going through to get there.

Secondly, transition will simply mean exactly as above but without the actual death of the physical body. So, if we are in transition in our life without being ill or dying, this will mean that a stagnated, at-a-crossroads feeling will occur within us and we can feel stuck and find ourselves searching for answers. Transition always feels awkward, but once a transition – no matter how big or small – has gone through the correct energetic process, transformation will kick in and we will feel in flow and in positive vibrational frequency.

Vibrational Frequency – This is all about energy, as you know, and the more you learn you will begin to understand your energy and other energies from the living and from spirit. This also includes energy from the land, trees, and plants, as well as animals. All energy holds a frequency which has a certain density. The vibrations we feel from particular energies will make us feel certain things, whether positive, neutral, or negative. There is no right or wrong with energy frequency, but we need to be aware that if something or someone in our lives is not on the same frequency to us, then it might not always feel good to be around them or to do certain things in our life. We also have our own thoughts and actions that do not align within our rightful vibrational frequency, so this is when crossroads will happen and we will feel confused about a particular area or person in our life.

Chapter 13

The Sunflower Signature...

You may have seen in my spiritual glossary the meaning of a spirit guide signature. If you didn't see that part, then please go and read it, because this will help you to understand what I am talking about.

I mention in Chapter One about a particular guide that I started to speak to in my mind when I was going through a very hard time in my life; her name was Mellie, and she was the most beautiful courageous woman. She was the best friend that my mum ever had, and they were like sisters. I always viewed her as a second mum, as we were very close and just had such a good bond. She guided me in life, and guidance is what she still gives me. She is now such a beautiful soul that connects with me often, and I feel her truth and her strength as she has helped me in so many ways through my life. She has been in the spirit realm for over nine years now.

Mellie's favourite flower was a sunflower, and at her funeral she wanted everyone to have a beautiful big sunflower to take away. That sunflower was the beginning of something magical regarding my connection with her. At the time of her passing, I was addicted to a drug-infused, intoxicated, destructive life, so even though I knew I was spiritual and had these spiritual senses, I did not really use them. I was very much stuck, and in a bad way. So, I didn't notice signs from Mellie for the first few years of her passing.

In Chapter One, I talked about the three to four-year process of clearing and healing that I went though, both physically and spiritually, that led me to be who I am today. It was during the third year of that healing process that I began to feel Mellie around strongly, and I would speak to her in my mind. I would sometimes see her, which would make me feel very loved and supported. This was the time in my life where I was no longer doing drugs or intoxicating myself, but I was struggling with the impact of the pain and carnage that my actions had brought.

I felt that I was waking up spiritually, and Mellie was the one that was waking me up. She felt like such a glowing, shining goddess when she would come through so brightly. Later on, after setting up my spiritual business, I was in a much better place. I had been working with allowing my life to be guided, so I was a lot more on top of my emotions and my life. What I found was that I would see flashes of sunflowers in my mind as an image, and it would immediately make me think of Mellie. At that time, I was aware of her and other guides that I had, and I had been delving enthusiastically into discovering my clairsensory system. Yet I was still not totally connecting a signature with Mel, and didn't really realise what a spirit guide signature was then.

I would find that my mum or my sisters would start talking about Mellie and how they were thinking of her, and I would say, 'That's interesting, so have I.' A light bulb started to go off in my brain, and I realised that every time I think of Mellie I see an image of sunflowers in my mind through my internal clear seeing clairvoyance. So, what she's really doing is providing me with her signature when she wants to connect with me. I felt so excited with this realisation, and I started to tune into this in meditation and worked with Mellie to understand her signature of the sunflower. As a result, the sunflower became special to me, because I knew it was my special guide helping me.

What then happened over the next five years – and is still ongoing now – were some of the most amazing situations, where sunflowers turned up in all manner of ways at just the right times, whether it was in moments of doubt, or some sort of difficult situation with family or friends that were linked to her and us, or whether it was significant to my business and my own personal life. No matter what, the sunflowers were there.

And over the years, many of my friends, students, members, and clients have given me sunflowers – some in a picture on Facebook, where they've tagged me, saying I remind them of a sunflower; or a drawing of a sunflower that someone did for me; and postcards and thank you cards with photos of sunflowers. My sister-in-law brought me a lovely sunflower hairband on the anniversary of Mellie's passing – without knowing it was that day. These were all amazing signs that the signature of my spirit guide was growing and becoming stronger, because I was believing and connecting more and more.

I also received bookmarks with sunflowers and a message saying, 'I feel you needed this', which usually landed at the best times possible. And some people actually brought me real sunflowers; no matter what other flowers were in the bunch, there were always sunflowers in there. As soon as I would see these flowers that people brought me, I just knew, *Ahhhhhh Mellie has guided them to do that for me.* Students have given me gifts of sunflower bags, bracelets, earrings, and necklaces on different occasions; it's just incredible.

The most recent sunflower signature sign was a truly magical one. I had been on the phone to a photographer, discussing some branding photos for my business, when I suddenly felt draw to tell him all about Mellie and the sunflower. And that is what led to us deciding on the front cover for this book. I also shared with this photographer that after eight years of being together, my partner and I had decided to set a date and book a venue for our wedding. In fact, we had done so earlier that day, so I was pretty excited.

I could most definitely feel Mellie around me during this photography branding call and we decided to definitely include sunflowers into my branding and into the book, as well as my Tarot deck. I came off that call feeling super excited and carried on with my work.

Later that evening, I was actually in my dressing gown, getting ready to chill for the evening with my family when there was a knock at the door. I was confused because it was nearly 8pm and we weren't expecting anyone. At the door was one of my newer students. I invited her in, and she said she had felt drawn to get me something earlier that day, and that she really was sorry for turning up unexpectedly but that she couldn't wait to give it to me. Obviously, it's always lovely getting a treat, so I opened it excitedly and there, sure enough, was a beautiful cup with a huge sunflower on. This to me was the icing on the cake after such an amazing day of booking our wedding and having that great branding call.

I knew that Mellie had guided my student to buy that cup for me to show me a huge sign that she had been listening to my conversation and that she knew about setting my date. When I asked my student what had guided her to pick the sunflower one, she said she just felt that I had to have it. When I told her everything that the sunflower meant to me and what had been going on, she looked shell shocked.

I am ever so grateful to see Mellie connecting to my students and regular clients to guide them in some way, whether that is to give me a sign or to help them in their own lives. Not long after that, another student sent me an image of a sunflower wedding cake. This student didn't realise that we plan to have sunflowers as our main theme and that the cake will have sunflowers on. So this was another sign.

This has been such a lovely uplifting signature, which so many of them will be, because signature should be warming and loving. But my journey exploring and understanding this signature and letting it unfold has been absolutely mind-blowing, to the point where so many people have been involved, whether they realised it or not.

So, if you're reading this and you know that you have tagged me in a sunflower post or gifted me something sunflower-themed, then you now know that you have been a part of something much bigger. You have been a part of my journey and of the magic that is THE SUNFLOWER SIGNATURE OF MELLIE.

Mellie: You are my sunflower. You shine so bright, you guide me with your love, and I appreciate you. I love you and I am ever grateful for your glow. Thank you for my sunflowers, thank you for your energy, and thank you for knowing my contract and helping me to complete my contract of life.

Melanie Lago Worman,
July 29th, 1953 – August 21st, 2011

Chapter 14

Amazing Ancestors

Well, what can I say? The journey of meeting some of my ancestors has been amazing, with so many incredible examples of guidance. It is important not to be fixated on your guides only being loved ones that you knew, because we have so many ancestors that are waiting to connect with us. They are our family, even if we never physically knew them. And that is why when ancestors come through, sometimes people dismiss them because they don't realise that they are actually their guide. We just have to listen and assess, using our clairs, exactly what it is they are showing us. And when you start delving into your ancestors, this is such a precious and amazing energy, because the significance can be mind-blowing. You may feel bonded to one or some of them and not understand why, because you never knew them, but your soul knows them. And you have been with them time and time before, in many lifetimes, hence the reason there are bonds that can sometimes feel so strong.

My first memory of actually meeting some ancestors was very strong. I was doing a meditation where I went into a house which looked like my grandma's (she was still alive at the time). There were some parts of the house I didn't recognise, but I had a strong knowing that I knew this house. Inside, I went into the left-hand room and I saw an older man with grey hair, a moustache, smoking a pipe, and playing a grand piano. He was very theatrical and funny, and I liked him.

I went back into the hallway and walked into the right-hand room. Now this room was very grand with high ceilings – totally different to the first room, which felt very small. I was drawn to look out of the large window, and outside I saw a younger man in a white cricket outfit in the fields beyond the main garden. It was a very old-fashioned cricket outfit that felt very prominent to me in this meditation.

As I was looking out of this grand window, I felt very sad, and I became aware of someone standing behind me. I turned back to the middle of this lovely room, and there was a beautiful lady there with brown hair up in a very posh bun, wearing a black buttoned-up, corseted dress, and a pearl necklace. She looked very grand, but I felt she was sad but strong. She just stared at me and I felt so connected to her. I didn't think to ask her who she was, because I was so amazed at all this detail I was seeing. I knew she was going to help me, though.

I eventually left this house and came out of meditation knowing something amazing had taken place. I immediately rang my mum to tell her about my experience. Mum thought it was amazing, but she couldn't place who the cricket man and the lady were. What she could place was the man at the piano with the pipe, who she said was my great-great-grandfather, George, my Grandma Meryl's grandfather. She could also place the house that I had seen, which still exists to this day.

This manor house is the home my grandma grew up in, so a long string of my ancestors have lived there. I couldn't understand how I did not know this, but I guess it was because I never thought to ask. I felt very excited that my ancestors had taken me all around their home and that there was such strong significance to everything I had been shown. So, I knew that something special was happening. The reason why I was seeing different types of rooms is because I was actually being shown how the rooms changed over centuries of my ancestors living there.

It took many months before I discovered who that beautiful woman was, even though I saw her again several times. About three weeks after that first connection with the woman in that house, my Grandma Meryl passed away, but it wasn't until about six months after she passed that Mum decided to go through all Grandma's old photos. I picked up my phone one day and opened a message from my mum to see a photo of the lady I had seen so powerfully, in the exact outfit she wore when I first saw her, and her hair styled in the same way. I was absolutely astounded to finally have clarity on who she was. It turns out she is my great-great-grandmother, who was married to the man I saw by the piano. So, you see, sometimes we have to wait for clarity, but when it comes it is so significant.

After that, Mum and I decided to look into our family tree, and sure enough there was the cricket man in the picture wearing the same cricket outfit. He was my great-great-grandfather George, and had been showing me a younger version of himself in my meditation.

Alongside all of this, I had also had a connection with another man who I knew was also an ancestor. This came about two weeks after my grandma passed, when I was standing in my mum's kitchen and became aware of a man speaking to me. He was saying, 'Bertie, Bertie' but that his name was Harold, and he was with Bertie. When I told my mum, she said it was my great uncle Harold; he and the others used to call my grandma Bertie, because her maiden name was Burton. My mum also explained that my great uncle Harold was a medium and ran a spiritual centre way back. Again, I was pretty gobsmacked and couldn't believe I never knew this, but I guess sometimes when we're young we don't think to ask.

I began to connect to these lovely ancestors more and more, and I realised why the connection was stronger after my grandma passed. It was because they wanted to continue the Burton energy through the DNA of the Burton ancestral line. Harold in particular helps me with my mediumship, and I have had an amazing journey listening to him on a deeper level to continue the psychism and mediumship strength going through the family line. I now have a deeper understanding of why I am meant to be a medium, because it runs through our blood. My great-great-grandma helps me with healing and to heal family past issues, while my great-great-grandfather George reminds me to stay playful and to continue to focus in a fun way on what I'm doing.

Through these connections I have had some unbelievable messages and guidance that have helped me to grow and improve upon my life, my business, and my family DNA. This is why I feel it is so important to understand and learn your family tree, so that you can use your ancestral energy to continue forward with your journey. Especially if you are a medium, use their messages to guide you, because they truly care about you. Their connections are not just random spirit popping in. There will be a significant reason, and it's down to you to understand this significance.

To my ancestors, I thank you for all that you have taught me. I thank you for your energy and support, I thank you for the Burton DNA, and I honour you. I will continue to live out your energy through me, and continue your amazing work. I love you.

Great-great-grandfather George Burton.
Great-Uncle Harold Burton.
Great-great-grandmother Emma Lena Burton.

Chapter 15

Meryl Watson – Grandma

My lovely, amazing grandma, Meryl Watson, was a wonderful woman, with such a story to tell. She was the only grandmother I ever knew physically, and I have such fond memories of her. Grandma was very much into the spiritual world, and she and my grandfather used to run spiritual classes and talks a long time ago when such things were considered weird and crazy.

In her last years of life, my grandmother most definitely had all her marbles right up until the end, and she always loved to ask me how I was getting on with my development and my business. She passed about a year into my business being off the ground. She was always very proud of me, and I loved seeing her face light up when I would tell her what I was achieving. We would also have conversations about the spirit that she was seeing and being drawn to, and I would connect to them as well. It was truly magical to have this bond and to know she had my back – and, oh my gosh, she certainly did.

She has been such a source of guidance since her passing on 6th December, 2017. Every time she connects and visits with me, I say, 'Wow, Grandma, what have you been up to? You are glowing and seem even lighter than before.' She shows me what she's been doing and who she has been visiting. She also gives me guidance of what's coming up for me.

It feels that when she passed, she left a huge amount of positive energy with me that shifted my spiritual awareness to the next level. My senses stepped it up in such a huge way, and they have just become stronger and stronger since.

As I shared earlier in the book, the day she passed was one I will never forget. She had fallen asleep for about a week and unfortunately had some sedation, so the doctors informed us that she most likely wouldn't wake up. Each time I visited her during that week, I could see her spirit body slowly coming out of her physical body, so we knew it wouldn't be long before she passed to the spirit realm. On the day she did pass, I had this awful feeling of grief and I couldn't shake it off. My dog was attached to my side all day and I knew he was sensing that there was going to be a passing soon. For weeks, the whole family had been wondering whether that would be the day it would happen, so we were all a bit on edge.

I remember coming through my hallway into the kitchen while I was on the phone. I was already staring in the direction of the kitchen window as I came through the hallway, and noticed a magpie sitting on the window ledge. Now, we never get magpies outside the house – especially right on the ledge – so I knew there and then that Grandma was passing later that day. I told my partner on the phone that it was happening that day, then quickly rang my mum. She had to take her car for its M.O.T. so I said that I would go to be with Grandma.

Waiting for my partner to get home from work so that

he could watch the girls and let me leave was terrible. I just knew she was going to pass over and I had all these thoughts rushing through my head: *What if she dies before mum gets back? What if I'm on my own with her when she dies? I can't see her dying, but I want to be with her dying*. It was such a mess of emotion.

I had made tomato soup for me and the girls to eat before their dad got back, but I just couldn't stomach it. I knew what the evening was going to entail. As soon as my partner was home, I headed over to the manor home where Grandma was. I pulled up in the car and sat there for about ten minutes, trying to find the strength to go in.

I signed into the reception at 18:24, climbed the stairs to the top floor, and entered her room. There was a nurse sitting with her which was nice, and it felt peaceful. As the nurse left the room to make me a cup of tea, I looked at my grandmother and said, 'Oh Grandma, this is really it, I know you're going.' I felt there wasn't much time and was worried that the nurse would bring me the cup of tea whilst Grandma was taking her last breath.

As she handed me the cup of tea and left the room, Grandma's breathing totally changed, and I realised that she had been waiting for the nurse to leave the room so that there would be no interruptions whilst she was passing. I suddenly thought of my mum and how devastated she would be if she wasn't here in time, so I had to assess whether to try and ring Mum or to tune into how long Grandma had left. I tuned in and was told it was a matter of minutes.

I stroked Grandma's hand and sent her love, knowing I was helping to assist her over to the spirit realm. I told her that it was ok, that she could go, and that we would look after Mum, and with that I watched Grandma take her last breath. It was amazing but so sad seeing that last gentle breath move through the whole of her body... and then nothing. The silence was deafening. I put my hand to her heart, and it was so still. Grandma had left her body.

I knew my great-grandparents, Mellie, and other ancestors, were all there with us and I knew that Grandma was standing out of her body and seeing me with her physical body. The time of her passing was 18:34 – exactly ten minutes after I'd signed into the building. Even though there had been little time with her, those moments have lasted with me as if it were yesterday.

I spent that time with Grandma playing her some of her favourite music and waiting for my mum and sister to arrive. Of course, Mum was devasted that she hadn't been there, and it has been something that she has had to work through, but she was glad that I had been with Grandma. I spent many months afterwards, wondering why it ended up being me that was with Grandma when she passed, and what I got was that it was a gift from my ancestors to be able to witness that. I understand now that if I am always connecting to spirit, it was a lesson to actually watch and be wholly with someone you love whilst they cross over. I understand that it was that final physical sign Grandma gave me.

After that night, my senses became even stronger, and I left knowing I had received some sort of amazing energy that started to work its way through me, and has continued over the years.

As I said earlier, my grandma has sure been busy since

she reached the other side. She has really been making the rounds and enjoys it, and she is most certainly a loved one that gives huge signs. She has guided me in my business any time I have been worried about something or needed something, whether it be emotionally, physically, financially, or energetically, and has brought me a great deal of comfort and strength.

My business has grown with her guidance and I know and can feel that she is still so proud of me. My connection with her over the past three years has grown even stronger and I know that she and Mellie have connected in the spirit realm and have sometimes worked together to help me on various projects or goals.

About two months after Grandma's passing, she came to me, showing me a book. I kept seeing parts of the front cover were yellow, and she told me I must write a book. These images, thoughts, and feelings about writing a book became stronger until one day in March 2019, I was driving home from the group that I taught, and she said again, 'Write this book.'

I told her, 'Grandma, I'm writing, but I don't know how to write a book. I don't know where to begin or who to even speak to about getting a book published. So, if you want me to write this book you keep showing me, I'm listening, but you have to show me a sign of what action to take and make me take this action.'

I arrived home late and went straight to bed. The next morning, I woke up and, whilst still in bed, I had a little peek on Facebook. For some reason, I ended up on a networking group that someone had added me into ages before, but I had never really looked on it properly. I found myself watching a lady called Cassandra Farren discussing on a Facebook live about why writing a book is so beneficial for you in all manner of ways. The lightbulb was clicking, and I realised, *Holy fuck, Grandma, that was fast work with that sign!*

At the end of this discussion, Cassie let people know about an opportunity that she was working on and how she would be offering writing mentoring during this event. I immediately signed up, excited to get started and ready for the event later that year in October. Unfortunately, I didn't get to meet Cassie at that event, but I did write a chapter for a collaboration book – and that was the start of my writing journey, which Grandma has been guiding me through.

Of course, I knew that I was still going to be writing my own book, but this chapter helped me to understand the writing process and to meet people who would end up helping me. That particular collaboration book hit number one in Amazon's best seller category on the 6th of December – the anniversary of Grandma's passing. It was the most bittersweet day, and I just knew that she had guided me to be involved with that.

The following March, I found myself being pulled intensely to get into writing my own book, but I still had the problem of who would publish my book. I meditated and met Grandma in the space of white light, and told her, 'Grandma, I'm confused. Who do I get to publish my book? Please show me.' She told me to go back to the beginning.

I was a little confused at first, because I couldn't understand which beginning. The beginning when Cassandra Farren was shown to me? Suddenly it all flooded in, and I remembered that March morning the previous year when I'd watched the Facebook live that Cassie had been chatting in. And I realised that she was who Grandma was guiding me towards to help publish my book. It felt so right emotionally that I picked up the phone and messaged Cassie.

She didn't know me from Adam; we had never physically met and had never actually spoken. So I was aware that I was going to tell her all of this stuff about Grandma telling me to publish my book with her, but she might not believe in this type of thing. However, I trusted my grandma. When I called Cassie, I explained the whole process of why I wanted to speak to her, and I could just tell that the energy was great. I was crying, and Cassie was crying, and it was just so moving!

That is where my publishing journey began and, you guessed it, Cassie sure as hell published my book, as well as getting me to write a chapter for her collaboration book, *The Girls Who Refused to Quit*! I know my grandma would like Cassie. Grandma saw through people, so she knew exactly who was genuine and who was not, and she is still protecting and guiding me to authentic, kind people who are in alignment with what I'm trying to achieve.

The movement of the spiritual motions that she brings is absolutely astounding, and her energy continues to amaze me. You see, the energy of your soul purpose, and the people, places, and opportunities that are meant to happen, start to come in sometimes years before the actual moment. Grandma was working with another aspect of my life long before I fully realised. It's only now that I can see that her guidance was coming to me about a year before I realised it. It was, in fact, around the same time I went to that writing retreat in Marbella that I mentioned earlier, then I flew straight to Mexico after.

In Mexico, whilst I was writing my first chapter of that first collaboration book, I found myself feeling a stronger sense of purpose and starting to be surrounded by more and more positive people who were on an aligning energy frequency to me. Whether that be friendships, or working relationships, or clients, it was all beginning to flow so much more.

One day, I took a break from writing and was sitting in the sun by the beautiful beach, just having a nosey on Facebook. Someone had shared a live video which I was drawn to watch, and involved a lady called Michelle Stonhill. I had started watching the stream halfway through, so was just getting the gist of what she was talking about, and I gathered she was a business coach. Putting all that aside, I felt very drawn to her. I liked her energy and what she was saying. I remember saying to my partner, who was cuddled up next to me, 'Look at this lady. I like her vibe and I would love to meet her.' But then we put our phones down, carried on cuddling and watching the waves, then continued with the rest of the day.

I forgot all about that live stream and that lady I had felt drawn to, and in the following months my life went from strength to strength, my business continued to thrive, and other fabulous opportunities and connections with spirit continued.

The following August, I did a reading for a lovely lady, who said she really enjoyed it. A few weeks later, she sent me some information about a self-employed spiritual opportunity, and said she felt that I should check it out. So, I gave thanks and checked out the details of this opportunity. At first, I wasn't going to, because I was already very busy with my own business and wasn't sure whether I could take anything else on. But then my grandma kicked in and said, 'You MUST apply!' So I vibed in, it felt good, and I applied.

The process involved sending over your business links and information, and if the company liked the look of you, they'd invite you to do a reading for someone in the company. I was picked for the first stage and did a reading for the C.E.O.'s Personal Assistant, who was just a lovely soul, and she decided to put me through to the second stage. I would then be doing a reading for the C.E.O. of the company that I would be working for if I was successful.

I was one of three people, out of hundreds who applied, that got through to the stage of reading for the C.E.O. As soon as I got on the call, I felt very comfortable, because I believe that we are all equal, so I was just myself. During the reading, I kept feeling like I recognised her. I couldn't place where from, but I felt such a magnetic pull.

During the first reading round with her P.A., I had picked up that a person close to her had lost a baby girl. She confirmed this but did not give me any further information. Then, during the reading with the actual C.E.O., I began to feel the same energy of that baby girl coming through, and I realised that it was actually the C.E.O. that had lost a baby girl. So, I connected more with her baby's energy and picked up lots of things.

When the reading ended, I was told that there would be another call, which would be a chance for the C.E.O. to get to know me and my business better, and to see if I would fit in with what she wanted to achieve for her company.

A few days later, as I was standing in my kitchen, I felt the lady's baby girl coming back to me. She kept saying, 'Can you tell my mummy that I'm here, and my name is Ella.' I said to Ella, 'I can tell her, but I don't usually say stuff to people outside of a reading setting, because I believe it should be their choice to approach me for guidance.' Ella, though, was very persistent, so I decided to message the C.E.O.

I thought she might be annoyed at me, but I was so drawn to tell her, so I voice-clipped her exactly what I had felt and heard, then left it at that. Later on, I had a response from the C.E.O. to say that she was blown away, because that is the name she and her husband had chosen for their baby. She also said that on the day I messaged her she had been feeling really low about her pregnancy/baby/mother journey, and receiving my message had shifted her to feel more positive again. So, the message had come at the exact right time for her.

The energy of how these messages come through is just so amazing, and also so healing and reassuring, so I felt very blessed and happy with my decision to contact her. After this connection, I began to have some big realisations and more things started to click into place. Grandma was really around me so much, and I kept wondering why the C.E.O.'s name – Michelle Stonhill – seemed so familiar. It was actually my partner who reminded me that she was the one we'd seen on the video while in Mexico the previous October, and I'd said I would love to meet her.

Suddenly it all came flying back to me. HOLY FUCK – I FUCKING DID!! But why did I forget about that? Grandma said, 'Because you had to be guided into this opportunity at the exact right time.' I was stunned. That had been almost a whole year before; it was insane. But I realised that on that day on the beach, I had been shown a little snippet of someone that I would definitely meet in the future, but actually work with, too.

About a week later, I received a message from Michelle telling me that I had been chosen for the position of Spiritual Connection Coach within her company. I was over the moon and I knew 100% that this was written into my soul contract and that my grandma was guiding me and Michelle together, which was why I had felt such a strong magnetic pull. I told Michelle about the synchronicities that had taken place and she said she felt the same.

I know that this next part of my journey within Michelle's company is going to be magical and exciting, and is another stage of my spiritual journey. And it is yet another amazing example of my beautiful grandma guiding me, and how the energy of our soul contract actually kicks in a long time before we even realise. Everything is divinely timed perfectly.

I love you, Meryl Watson, my beautiful grandma. The lessons you taught me whilst alive and now in spirit have been the most amazing lessons ever. I hear you, I feel you, I see you, Grandma. Thank you for your energy. Thank you for being my guiding light. Thank you for always having my back. I feel your true love. I know you are there. I love you.

Meryl Auwdsley Watson
– December 17th, 1921 – December 6th, 2017

And finally...

So, that brings us to the end of this part of our journey together of exploring a deeper connection to your spirituality. I've loved sharing the techniques I have created so that you can explore each clairsensory within your energy stream. I hope that you have enjoyed discovering how to remain protected and grounded as you gain more control of your spirituality.

I hope that I am leaving you feeling inspired, along with a knowing of why you felt guided to pick this book up. Feeling clearer on your own path of spiritual discovery is amazing, but remember it is down to you to do the work. There is a lot to take in, but my advice is to go back and practise the practical exercises on a regular basis. Step-by-step, day-by-day, everything will become clearer.

At times it may feel as though you are taking three steps forward and one step back... trust this is part of the healing process and keep going.

Be proud of who you are.

Ignite Your Light, and never stop shining.

Love Elly x

About the Author

Elly Charles is a well known Psychic Medium & Spiritual Coach she is the founder of the company Light After Life where she runs her spiritual courses focusing on many aspects of spirituality. Elly has a keen interest in mediumship and the clair senses which has led her to develop her signature courses providing mediumship and clair strengthening techniques. Elly has a reputation for accuracy and has developed a wide psychic and mediumistic skillset which means that her readings and teachings are often profound and transformative. As a result she has a global following.

Elly also runs her membership The School of Spirituality which reaches out to people far and wide again helping many to transform and discover their own spiritual path in life. You can find access to this in the contacts page.

Elly is also a proud mummy to Minnie and is a loving partner too. Elly takes pride in her family and teaching her daughter how to understand in her psychic senses. Elly states that having her daughter changed her life forever in the right way and her daughter is what motivates her every day to continue focusing on this life and business that she loves so much.

Elly has been nominated in The Soul & Spirit Magazine for best psychic and has celebrity clients seeking her spiritual guidance. Elly believes that ego can get in the way of being authentic and true in spiritual work. So she is always conscious of seeing the true unique beauty in everyone regardless of their status.

Elly comes from a family who for generations had psychic and mediumistic abilities using them for the good of all, so it is only natural that she began developing those skills early in life. Elly learned from her mother and grandmother, who has since become one of her guides in spirit.

Later in life Elly also trained with a number of mediums, each giving her valuable guidance towards her own mediumship. She has also studied at The Arthur Findlay College several times, the School of Psychics and the International Academy of Consciousness where she attended intensive out of body training.

Elly believes that that the most powerful energy in the universe is LOVE. There is always help and support from spirit and from higher realms. She also believes that dark times in our lives are there for us to learn and grow. It was through her own dark times experiences that she discovered the love from her ancestors in spirit. Elly was able to see and trust the light that guided her towards her spiritual path. As a result of her trusting in this energy she has now been able to help thousands of people find their own path through her readings, courses and spiritual coaching.

Elly feels so blessed to have a following that supports her business and truly sees the love that surrounds Light After Life and her wonderful School of Spirituality. Having helped so many amazing people gain clarity on not only their spiritual senses but also on their lives is truly life transforming.

Elly believes that when we are having an awakening and then aligning everything in our lives becomes clearer. Everyone is different but what we all have in common is that WE ARE ALL ENERGY. Energy is what moves us forward into enlightenment.

To find out more about Elly please check out her website, The School of Spirituality membership or head over to her facebook and Instagram via the links on the contact page.

Contact Elly

Website
https://ellycharlesmediumship.com/

The School of Spirituality
https://ellycharlesmediumship.com/spirituality-2/

Facebook Business page
https://www.facebook.com/ellycharlesmediumship

Instagram
https://www.instagram.com/elly_charles_psychicmedium/

Facebook
https://www.facebook.com/elly.charles/

Acknowledgements

I would like to acknowledge my partner Steve Taylor for supporting me from start to finish with my writing journey. I will never forget sat on the beach in Mexico you were the first one to read my opening chapter and the first to read anything written of mine. Thank you so much for loving and supporting me. I love you with all my heart.

I want to acknowledge our daughter Minnie Taylor my beautiful ray of light. For Minnie you are what keeps me going and you are the reason I do everything in my life. I love you Minnie.

I want to thank my step daughter Kiera for all the lessons I have learnt from meeting you and yet we still have an awesome bond. Thank you for being your beautiful self. I love you Kiera.

I want to thank my twin sister Bib Charles for forever being ready to help whenever I was having a meltdown. Bib you keep me strong and I am so grateful for that. I love you my twinettey soul sista.

I would like to thank my sisters Amy Lewis, Zoe Charles, Naomi Charles and my brother Dan Charles for always believing in me through thick and thin no matter how crazy life may have got they always knew I would come out feeling more positive in the end. Love you my family.

I would like to thank the Taylor family for always wanting to support me and Steve no matter what our journey has brought to us. Thank you for accepting me into your life and into your family.

I want to thank my Sunflower Spirit Guide Melanie Lago Worman for showing me sunflowers exactly when I need reassurance or guidance in the next steps of my life. Mellie I hear you, I see you, I love you.

I would like to also thank my beautiful friends Stephanie Dawson, Jessica Wilce, Lucy Farbrother, Polly Cole, Terri Morgan, Vikki Baglin, Casey Thomas and Lucy Rowells for all the times we have shared together some dark and some happy but we always made it through together. I want to thank you for always having my back and knowing me inside out. Thank you my girls for always telling me how proud of me you are. I am proud of you all too. I love you with all my heart.

I want to thank Lisa Wadley-Boulton, Georgie Christopher and Lisa Ormonde for when I met you, you girls brought me back to life in a time I needed to live again. Thank you for waking me up. Love you girls.

I want to thank my beautiful friend Tina Jones for always loving me and accepting me. Love you girl.

I would like to acknowledge Melody Harper for being my first ever one to one student and now my good friend. You kick started a new part of my journey that is still ongoing, and you inspire me every day. I love you loads.

I would like to thank Alison Roberts and Norma Little for being so much fun in my first ever daytime class, still years on you are not only my students but now my friends. Thank you for your ongoing support and your fun beautiful energy.

I want to thank every single student I have ever taught, past, present and future for trusting in me to guide you and teach you. I am so thankful to so many students all over the world for without you I wouldn't have my teaching career.

I want to thank each and every client I have ever had whether they just had one session or regular sessions for it was you guys that recommended me and helped me to share my skillset to more and more people and continue doing what I love so much.

I would like to thank all the girls from the previous collaborations books I have been in. For you girls started my writing journey with me. A special thanks to Rachael Barnes you know exactly what to say at the exact right time I am so grateful I met you.

I would like to thank each and every soul passed over that has ever connected to me, for when you connected you helped me to become a stronger better medium, ever growing and developing. To connect to each soul passed on is truly a blessing and I feel this love every day. You helped me to be the medium I am today.

I would like to thank each person that reads this book whether it be now or ten years from now. Thank you for taking the time to read my story and to learn my teachings.

I acknowledge Cassandra Farren at Welford Publishing for the publication of this book and the ongoing support with my writing. Wow what a journey we have shared together.

I acknowledge Natasha Holland at Natasha Holland Photography for my beautiful photo for my front cover and all your positive creative energy towards my book.

Thank you to Natasha Edwards and Jo Jo Ellen at

Femalepreneurs Academy for all your business support, helping me with strategies and soul plans to continue moving forward along my journey in the right way. Your coaching has truly been transforming. Thank you for always reminding me to believe in myself.

Thank you to Ellen Williams for all your support towards promoting this book.

Thank you to Nathan King for creating my books funnel and advertisement.

Thank you to my editor Christine Mc Pherson

Thank you to Jen Parker at Fuzzy Flamingo for typesetting my book and creating the front cover.

And lastly Thank you to all the Spiritual Soul Searchers out there for sharing my journey.

Elly's books

Elly has written a chapter in each of these collaboration books:

Rise of the Mumpreneur

The Girls Who Refused to Quit – Volume 2

The Elevation of the Femalepreneur – Volume 2

Available from Amazon.

Printed in Great Britain
by Amazon

67115068R00133